DEAL

POWER

DEAL

POWER

6
FOOLPROOF STEPS
TO MAKING DEALS
OF ANY SIZE

MARC DIENER

AN OWL BOOK

HENRY HOLT AND COMPANY • NEW YORK

Henry Holt and Company, Inc. / *Publishers since 1866*
115 West 18th Street / New York, New York 10011

Henry Holt ® is a registered
trademark of Henry Holt and Company, Inc.

An application for trademark registration for the name "Deal Power"
is pending with the United States Patent & Trademark Office.

The author gratefully acknowledges the following for permission
to quote from previously published material:
"Rumi: We Are Three," translation by Coleman Barks. Athens, GA:
Maypop Books, 1987. Copyright © Coleman Barks.
Excerpt from the screenplay for *Out of Africa* courtesy of Universal Pictures.

Library of Congress Cataloging-in-Publication Data
Diener, M. (Marc)
Deal power : six foolproof steps to making deals of
any size / Marc Diener.—1st ed.
p.   cm.
Includes bibliographical references (p.   ) and index.
ISBN 0-8050-4108-7 (pbk. : alk. paper)
1. Negotiation in business.   2. Contracts.   I. Title.
HD58.6.D54   1997
658.4'052—dc21   97-21591

Henry Holt books are available for special promotions and
premiums. For details contact: Director, Special Markets.

First Edition 1997

Designed by Victoria Hartman

Printed in the United States of America
All first editions are printed on acid-free paper. ∞

1   3   5   7   9   10   8   6   4   2

To everyone who has ever rushed
into a business deal and later regretted it.

A friend remarks to the Prophet, "Why is it
I get screwed in business deals?
It's like a spell. I become distracted
by business talk and make wrong decisions."

Muhammad replies, "Stipulate with every transaction
that you need three days to make sure."

Deliberation is one of the qualities of God.
Throw a dog a bit of something.
He sniffs to see if he wants it.

Be that careful.

Sniff with your wisdom-nose.
Then decide.

—*Maulana Jalal al-Din Rumi (1207–1273)*

CONTENTS

LIST OF FIGURES

WHY YOU SHOULD

READ THIS BOOK

The obscure we see eventually, the completely
apparent takes longer.

—Edward R. Murrow

Have you ever cut a good deal . . . the kind you really want to brag about? Maybe you got a great price, or a special favor, or were especially clever. Remember how good it felt to get what you really wanted? Maybe it wasn't just a good deal, but a *great* deal, one that left those on the other side just as excited as you. Those deals are exhilarating and inspiring, rare visions of the Brotherhood of Business acting in harmony.

Now, have you ever made a really *bad* deal? Admit it. We all have. Oh sure, you thought it was O.K. at the time. But then . . . you start thinking. "How come I didn't ask for this!" "Why didn't I think of that?" Your afterthoughts bounce around like bingo balls in a wire cage. The rattling gets louder and louder. "How could I have been so stupid?!" "My God, I've been taken, I've been chumped . . . *I've been had!*"

Whenever we buy, sell, trade, option, rent, lease, license, employ, or partner, we become deal makers. And deal making engages us on every level. It demands that we juggle data and establish priorities. It challenges us to brainstorm alternatives and forge alliances. It tries our tact and maturity, as well as our shrewdness at penetrating subterfuge. It tests our mettle, our nerve, our resolve, and even our ability to predict the future.

▪ ▪ ▪

Obviously, to me deal making is much more than some academic pastime. It's what puts wood in my fireplace and bread on my table. To date, I've earned my living as a lawyer who analyzes, negotiates, and drafts deals for all kinds of people and companies, primarily in the entertainment industry. I've seen bad deals ruin careers and I've seen good ones make them. It was this experience that led me to write this book. I'll explain.

You probably know that "players" in the entertainment game deal for everything. Agents make deals to represent actresses, writers make deals to collaborate, and musicians make deals to form pop groups. Producers make deals for stars, banks make deals to finance films, and studios swap scripts, facilities, and film libraries. "A-players" negotiate for real estate, health clubs, retirement condos for their parents, airplanes, exotic pets . . . you name it. And international magnates, tycoons, and moguls buy what they want, when they want it.

Some of these deals are unique to the entertainment industry. Most are not. After all, a license is a license, a purchase is a purchase, and a partnership is a partnership, whether or not a celebrity is involved. Over the years, I've done more than my share of deals. And over the years I noticed that no matter what kind of deal, no matter what the parties are dealing for, the same kinds of questions always come up:

"Is this deal really worth it?" "How do I check out the other side?" "How can I be sure they've got the money?" "What do I do if they don't?" The subject matter, the complexity, the sophistication of the players might vary, but the basic pattern is always the same . . . kind of like a house. Every house has walls, a floor, a ceiling, doors, and usually, windows; even igloos, tepees, and caves share these qualities. This, I found fascinating.

But even more illuminating were the clients who came to me after the fact. Their deals had gone south; the other side had them in a chokehold; they had signed on the dotted line without thought or help. True, some had little choice. But often they were like architects who had left a wall, a door, or a ceiling out of the blueprint. After all, we usually get ambushed from the front. This, I found absolutely compelling!

If only there were a checklist for making deals, I thought. If only there were a framework detailed enough to keep you from missing something important but general enough for almost any transaction, a step-by-step approach . . . whether you're on familiar ground or not, whether you're buying a car or a house, whether you're forming a simple partnership or merging two Fortune 500 companies. Because I'm involved in so many different kinds of deals, I just *had* to find such a checklist.

So, I started to search, and I was astounded. Human society is based on exchange. This is the most deal-oriented age in history. America, the most entrepreneurial nation on earth, was built on deals, like the sale of Manhattan and the Louisiana Purchase. We pore over biographies of the great entrepreneurs; every parent drills their kids on the birds and bees of business; our MBAs are numb from courses in finance, accounting, marketing, and management; our bookstores and libraries are filled with self-help and how-to books on every conceivable topic. Yet I couldn't find one book, one course, or even a simple magazine article that had the skeleton key for making a good deal!

That's why I wrote this book.

In the process, I think I've found a dynamic yet easy-to-use approach that works in every business situation, a method that can benefit everyone: the Deal Power System. I believe that all deal making can be reduced to six basic steps:

- stepping back
- getting help
- checking things out
- minimizing risk
- negotiating
- writing it down

Of course, just naming the steps doesn't begin to do them justice. At each stage you'll ask yourself several, or perhaps, many questions. But here's the bottom line: You may spend more time on certain steps, you may combine them, you may not even do them in order. But if you ignore or miss a step, you're asking for it. You'll see what I mean.

■　■　■

First, a few disclaimers: Although this book will serve you better than many so-called experts, it is no substitute for good professional advice. Throughout, I've done my best to indicate those tasks that the layperson should not "try at home." Although I've tried to make sure that all factual information is current, accurate, and complete, I don't guarantee it. This is especially true with principles of law for which exceptions, qualifications, and conditions abound. Lastly, because there are no absolutes in deal making, no advice can apply to every situation.

If you're a beginner, I hope you find what follows to be clear, concise, and enlightening—commonsense tips to avoid the pitfalls and classic mistakes of deal making. Some information is a bit technical, such as the sections on backgrounding and legal due diligence, and some information may not be relevant to every deal, like that on hiring an attorney, accountant, or other pricey professional. The important things are the approach and the concepts. You may ultimately choose to disregard many suggestions, but if you consider *all* the questions, your decisions will be informed ones, and your success, satisfaction, and self-confidence at making business deals will increase.

To you specialists and aces out there: This is not just another anthology of war stories or tome on high-power haggling. There's a ton of information here and surely *even you* can pick up a thing or two. More importantly, this book can help organize what you do naturally. Even the most grizzled veteran misses things in the heat of battle. Here is your safety net. Maybe thumbing through the right chapter at a tough time will bust an impasse, check a bad move, or simply help you see the forest for the trees.

Above all, enjoy the process. Use this guide creatively. Here is your instruction manual to this most uniquely human of activities. For there are only three things that separate humans from beasts: their neocortices, their opposable thumbs, and most important . . . *their ability to make deals*!

ACKNOWLEDGMENTS

Above all, I thank my editor, David Sobel, for helping me conceive and write a better book than I could have written on my own. My thanks also to Jonathan Landreth, Eric Wybenga, and the other folks at Holt for their patience, professionalism, and responsiveness.

I am grateful to my agent, Al Zuckerman, for believing in me and my material.

For invaluable peer review and support, I am indebted to Michael Blaha, Jay Dougherty, Bob Gentino, Elisabeth Grace, Lee Gruenfeld, Mark Halloran, Brian Kingman, Bill Klein, Jan Krause, Ely Malkin, John Mills, Richard Parr, and Paul Sandberg. I also acknowledge James Cook, Corey Copeland, Conley Falk, Jeff Korchek, Leanna Johnson, Lisa Margolis, Mark Mastalir, Mark Maxey, and Jim Velutato for their help.

And, of course, Kristina, Alana, and Tilly ... the best deals I ever made.

DEAL

POWER

I

THE

DEAL POWER

SYSTEM

1

STEP 1:

STEP BACK (AND THINK)

Holy Kleenex, Batman! It was right under our nose and we blew it.

—Robin, the Boy Wonder

Like a fire, a deal can start in many ways. You may have a problem to solve, money to invest, expertise to sell, or an empire to build. Whether you're looking for action or it's looking for you, no matter how exciting, scary, aggravating, and wonderful it all is, there's one thing you must always do first:

TAKE THE TIME TO *THINK* ABOUT WHAT YOU ARE DOING!!

This may sound unbelievably obvious, but from time to time everyone forgets this simple principle. Whether we're too trusting, too greedy, too pressured, too proud, too uninformed, too lazy, or too optimistic, there is a natural tendency to rush into a deal, even for the most experienced. Want some high-profile examples? Take the dozens of disastrous corporate marriages of the 1980s. Here is an observation from a June 1985 *Business Week* article called "Do Mergers Really Work?": "The lessons seem clear. Mergers can work under the right circumstances. What is astonishing is that so few companies seem to have studied the historical evidence before plunging ahead." Later, John Duncan, then chairman of St. Joe Minerals Corporation, is quoted on his company's particularly ill-fated merger with Fluor; the time spent making the deal, he said, was "so brief it was embarrassing."

By the way, this is not just about some trend in Big Business in the late twentieth century. This is a universal human experience. Every

THE DEAL POWER SYSTEM IN A NUTSHELL

1. **Step back (and think)**
   Pull out your checklist
   Answer three threshold questions:
   Why am I doing this? (Goals)
   Does it seem like a good deal? (Value)
   What are my alternatives? (Creativity)

2. **Get help**
   Do I need an investment banker, attorney, accountant, appraiser, consultant, detective, agent, or broker?
   Have I used all available self-help resources, such as books, on-line services, libraries, and government programs to best advantage?
   Have I talked it over with someone I'm close to?

3. **Check it out**
   What impression does the other side make?
   Have I checked out the numbers?
   Have I run a background check?
   Have I checked out the legalities?

4. **Minimize risk**
   Have I taken control of the exchange, the length of the deal, and the other side's performance?
   Do I have collateral?
   Am I protecting my secrets?
   Have I gotten as many people on the hook as possible?
   Do I have all the insurance I need?
   Can I use a written contract to shift my risks?
   Have I protected my assets in case of a lawsuit?

5. **Negotiate**
   Do I know my bottom line?
   Have I analyzed who's got more power?
   Have I negotiated effectively?
   Is the other side fighting fairly?
   Am I being fair?
   Am I overdoing it?

6. **Write it down**
   Am I preparing the papers?
   Does my contract give me an edge?
   If I'm not preparing the papers, do they accurately reflect the deal?
   Am I keeping good files?

Fig. 1.1

person you meet can tell you about an important business deal they made too quickly and later lived to regret. I guarantee it.

So what is the antidote to impulsive, ill-conceived, and sloppy deal making? A checklist! Study figure 1.1 carefully. This is the skeleton of the Deal Power System in question form.

In theory we follow the natural time line of a deal, starting with initial inquiries; moving through team building, due diligence, and risk management; and closing with negotiation and a written agreement. In real life, few deals are so tidy and predictable. But, for best results, apply these concepts over and over in as many ways as you can at each stage of the game. This will all be a lot more obvious after you've finished this book.

So let's get to work. Making deals takes time, money, and energy. The first thing to do is to weed out the bad, the mediocre, and the wrong ones. See figure 1.2 for deals you should avoid. The rest of this chapter is devoted to three threshold questions:

1. Why am I doing this?   Goals
2. Will it be worth it?   Value
3. What are my alternatives?   Creativity

GOALS: WHY AM I DOING THIS?

First Doctor: I operated on him for appendicitis.
Second Doctor: What was the matter with him?
—Anonymous

Because I'm an occasional rock 'n' roll lawyer, the pop stars of tomorrow sometimes seek me out. The deals they're offered are rarely generous. Yet one desperate singer showed me a contract that redefined the term "serf" music, with provisions that would have made a feudal overlord blush. I'll spare you the details, but let's just say that in an exploitive industry, the document I had been asked to review symbolized a new low. I was frank with my client, saying, "It is mathematically impossible for you to make one nickel on this deal. Why bother?"

"But you don't understand," he pleaded with me. "I just *gotta* get a record deal!"

RED FLAGS: 10 DEALS TO AVOID

Deal makers are constantly bombarded with opportunities, but no one has the resources to check out every lead. Here are ten deals to approach with extreme caution:

1. *Any deal you don't fully understand.* If the other side won't take the time to explain, or you won't make the effort to comprehend, all the aspects of a deal, then don't do it. Also, study the formal contracts thoroughly, including the fine print. It may give the other side rights that would make you shudder.

2. *Any deal requiring lots of money up front.* Con games depend on that tiny window of opportunity between your giving and your getting to exploit your peak vulnerability.

3. *Any deal you're asked to do in a hurry.* When the other side is hurrying and hassling you, it's because they know if they let you think once, you're sure to think twice.

4. *Any deal with people you don't know or with companies you've never heard of.* In Step 3, we'll learn how to check out the other side. But if you try and come up dry, start worrying.

5. *Any deal that's set up like a pyramid scheme.* Some of these are legit. However, when a company immediately wants to sell you thousands of dollars of nonreturnable inventory while promising you unbelievable profits for all the people you sign up, look for the exit.

6. *Any deal involving a tax shelter.* The glory days of these deals are long gone. Make sure your deal has real economic purpose, independent of tax consequences.

7. *Any deal involving a person or company whose accountants, bankers, or lawyers have quit.* This is a classic sign that something fishy is going on.

8. *Any deal that comes through an unsolicited phone call.* Although there are many honest telemarketers, the Federal Trade Commission estimates that the illegal ones fleece the public for more than $60 billion a year. Watch for high-pressure tactics, refusal to send

Fig. 1.2 *(continued on following page)*

Fig. 1.2 *(continued)*

written material, premature requests for bank account or credit card numbers, required overnight delivery, or courier pickup of checks or money orders. Remember: With great opportunities, no one should need to cold call.

9. *Any deal in which you're being harangued, manipulated, or schmoozed.* Don't tolerate these below-the-belt tactics.

10. *Any deal that sounds too good to be true.* It probably is.

The Deal Maker's Hierarchy of Needs

Good deal making starts with a little introspection: You have to ask yourself what you *really* want, and *why*. If you're honest, the answer may surprise you. Psychologist Abraham Maslow theorized a *hierarchy of human needs*, starting with basic ones like air, water, food, shelter, and sleep; continuing through sex, safety, security, love, belonging, self-esteem, and praise from others; and going on to the higher needs for truth, order, justice, beauty, unity, effortlessness, and self-sufficiency. Let's adapt his scale (loosely) to deal making.

Basic Needs
In deal making, money is the universal need. Even the related desires for time, a service, or any kind of tangible or intangible property convert back to plain dollars and cents. Generally, these needs are easy to see and understand.

Personal Needs
In every human activity there are hidden psychological drives that compel and propel. They're more difficult to discern and far more intriguing to explore. Here's what I mean:

Freedom—A successful venture capitalist harvests his company to enjoy some free time.

Pride—Each deal a captain of industry makes must be bigger and more visible than the one before.

Thrills—A high-risk investor speculates in syndicated racehorses, motion pictures, or obscure stock derivatives.

Peer pressure—A Fortune 500 executive looks for takeover targets because everyone else is.

Self-esteem—A struggling writer signs with the first agent to come along. The writer knows the agent is weak, but at least now the writer can say that he's "represented."

Artistry—To work with her favorite director, a successful actress accepts a role for a quarter of her asking price.

Involvement—A retiring employee stays on as a consultant.

Revenge—A middle-aged executive leaves a company he feels has slighted him to launch a competing one.

Family—A young couple buys a home in a safe neighborhood and a good school district.

Fun—A wheeler-dealer loves the brainstorming, camaraderie, and hustle and bustle of putting deals together.

Bias and Ego

Just as our hidden needs affect our judgment, so do our biases, especially when it comes to taking risks in deals. We talk ourselves into deals we like by downplaying the downside. We gamble more for gain than for an equal benefit that prevents loss. With tough decisions, we may gather information frantically, then choose with our gut anyway. Let's face it: We are not as rational as we'd like to believe.

Of all biases, the most treacherous is often the successful businessperson's inflated belief in his or her own ability: ego. Confidence is one thing, arrogance another, and a hot streak or mastery in one industry or business never guarantees future success in another.

Deal Maker, Know Thyself

So much of our lives are lived on automatic pilot. Only the exceptional individual steps back to ask, "Why am I doing this?" Here are a few more questions that may help you discover your true motives and biases before you sit down at the bargaining table:

How will I feel after I do this deal?
How will I feel while I am making it?

What will I have after I do this deal that I don't have now?
What won't I have?

What do I like about this deal?
What don't I like about it?

Why should I do this deal?
Why shouldn't I?

Can I really pull off what I am hoping to?
What am I overlooking?

By really being candid with yourself, you may clarify your goals and push forward afresh. Or you may reject a deal, finding simpler ways, or other areas of your life, in which to satisfy your true needs. My point is this: You can't make your best deal if you don't acknowledge your biases and know what you really want.

VALUE: WILL IT BE WORTH IT?

> Everything is worth what its purchaser
> will pay for it.
> —Publilius Syrus (first century B.C.)

"Is it worth it?" is the deal maker's "To be or not to be." After all is said and done, whether or not a deal closes depends on how each side answers this seemingly simple but really frighteningly complex question. The following bare-bones discussion lays out the basic angles from which the deal maker can approach this question. The IRS, a lender, or an insurance company, for example, might look at things quite differently. No doubt, to really nail down your numbers, you'll need help from one or more of the experts we'll meet in Step 2 and you'll have to do a fair amount of research on the "going rate" in whatever market you're in. In any event, the more tools you have to measure value, the more likely you'll be to cut a sharp deal.

The Elements of Value

Naturally, every deal has an upside and a downside. The upside is in the dollar value of what you receive, its long-term potential, and the personal needs it fulfills for you. The downside is in the risks you assume, the deals you forgo because you're tied up with this one, the time and money spent putting it all together, and, of course, in what

---

THE UPSIDE AND DOWNSIDE OF DOING A DEAL

	Upside	Downside
Doing the deal	Benefits • dollar value • long-term potential • subjective value	Risks Opportunity costs Transaction costs What the other side wants

Fig. 1.3

you give to the other side. Before we take each component in turn, here's a little diagram:

Dollar Value

This is not as simple as you might think. There are literally dozens of ways to calculate a deal's dollar value, some better than others, each with weaknesses and each relevant in different situations. We can boil them down to four basic approaches:

Historical or book value we look to out of habit, even though it has little to do with economic reality. The original price may mean nothing today. Depreciation may make even the most valuable holdings seem worthless, or it may be taken too slowly to reflect true value. Also, with companies, a calculation based solely on the historic value of its assets won't reflect its worth as a functioning operation, or *going concern*, especially its *goodwill* (see below).

Fair market value, or the price at which an independent buyer and seller might strike a deal, is often a much better gauge of value but only if an *arms-length* buyer and seller actually exist. Even then, the price offered may not fully reflect something's value. Such may be the case with that old car of yours that still runs great.

Replacement value may be closely related to market value; it is loosely defined as what it would cost to replace, license, or re-create the item in question. However, the answer is not worthwhile unless that something can be replaced, licensed, or re-created.

Earning potential is a more sophisticated approach. Professional appraisers have developed many different formulas to compute this figure, usually by multiplying a company's projected annual profits or sales, after-tax earnings, or dividends by an accepted industry multiplier called a *cap rate*, or by discounting some estimate of future cash flows. As you might imagine, technical problems abound. For example, how earnings, profits, and the like are calculated may vary with the accountant; choosing the most appropriate cap rate can be tricky; the underlying assumptions on which such a valuation is grounded are crucial; and if there are no earnings, dividends, or cash flow, there's nothing on which to base such a calculation.

Let's take a simple example: You buy a school bus at one price, can sell it at another, can replace it at yet another, and can earn a certain amount with it over its useful life. You get a different dollar value depending on which approach you choose, and you choose the approach that best supports the price you want to pay or to receive.

■ ■ ■

A couple of interesting problems come up when you're buying or selling a business, as opposed to a discrete item. First, goodwill will likely be an integral part of your analysis. Its standard definition is the excess a buyer pays over the net value of a company's tangible assets. This doesn't do it justice. Often, out of convenience or ignorance, every conceivable intangible is lumped into goodwill: trademarks; secret formulas; customer lists; the assemblage of the location, equipment, and personnel into a working unit; the reputation and know-how of the owners; technical libraries; special systems for running the day-to-day business; and so on. In fact, in today's information economy, intellectual property and intangibles may represent the bulk of a business's value. Because many of these intangibles have distinct measurable values in their own right and because goodwill is neither depreciable nor deductible from a tax standpoint, it's important to allocate it carefully in the total purchase price. The details of how to do this are beyond the scope of this discussion, but the professionals you will undoubtedly engage in this situation should be aware of the issue.

Second, stock may be valued quite differently depending on the size of the block traded. Shares representing majority or liquidating control will demand a premium, whereas a minority interest (without such controls) in a closely held business may be steeply discounted. Even experts don't agree on how great these premiums or reductions ought to be.

Long-Term Potential

By this I mean objective benefits on which it's tough to place an immediate dollar value. This factor applies more to deals where the strategic advantage of an entire company or business opportunity is an issue (as opposed to deals for a particular asset or service). Although the questions in figure 1.4 are very general, they'll start you thinking on the right track:

EVALUATING THE POTENTIAL OF BUSINESS OPPORTUNITIES

About a Market
Are you dealing in a market that's large or small? Growing or shrinking? Highly concentrated or dispersed? Long-term or temporary?
Who dominates the market? Why?
Is it open to newcomers? What are the barriers to entry?
What is your competitive advantage?
Can you anticipate political, legal, technological, environmental, or economic events that will affect the particular industry or the market in general?

About a Product or Service
What need does the product or service satisfy?
What is the expected life of the product or service?
Why is it better than what's already out there?
Exactly who are your customers and how easily can you reach them?
How do they, or will they, like the product?
What are they, or would they be, willing to pay for it?
Will the company be able to develop related products or services?
What are its profit margins? How much will you need to sell to break even? To turn a profit?

About a Company
Financially, how solid is it right now?
What is its financial history?
What is its reputation with customers? In the business community?
Is it beating, or being beaten by, its competitors? Why?
Technologically, is the company a leader?
How much can the company grow?
How diverse is the company?
What are insiders doing?

Fig. 1.4 *(continued on following page)*

Fig. 1.4 *(continued)*

Who are its main customers? Who are its main suppliers?

What shape are its assets in?

How will the deal affect each division of the company: Marketing? Research and Development? Finance? Management? Manufacturing?

Are there potentially devastating lawsuits on the horizon?

About People

As individuals or as a management team, how great is their experience? Their skill? Their integrity? Their vision? Their motivation? Their commitment to future excellence?

How heavily are you relying on particular individuals? What will happen if they leave?

Are they well connected? Will they use those connections to help you?

Are there personal, political, or family issues that will affect their performance?

About Outside Reaction

How will the competition respond to your doing the deal?

How will the competition respond to your *not* doing the deal?

How will others in the business community react? Will the deal enhance your power or reputation? Will it put you in a better position to do the next deal?

Subjective Value

In a sense we've already explored this in "The Deal Maker's Hierarchy of Needs" on pages 7–8. Personally, what really turns you on about a deal? Will you work with good friends? Work from home? Visit your favorite city more often? Fulfill some lifelong dream? It may be impossible to assign a dollar value to these perks, yet their value to you is all too real.

Risks

Risks permeate deals, as they do almost everything in life, and as far as I know, we have yet to devise the intellectual framework that will identify them all. In some deals you'll recognize particular risks immediately, perhaps because of the people involved or the subject matter or structure of the exchange. In any event, deal makers are always subject to the perils of nature, current events, dishonesty, or their own or others' poor judgment or fallibility. Each of the six steps in the Deal Power System will help you manage risk better generally. In particular, Step 3 will help you uncover hidden risks, and Step 4 will suggest specific ways to handle them. For now, do your best, factoring the most important ones into your analysis. The questions just listed in figure 1.4 will also help.

Opportunity Costs

Opportunity costs are not just theoretical. The money you could have made doing a different deal is all too real, as are the seemingly always greener pastures along the road not taken. To know the value of an opportunity, you must also know the value of its alternatives.

Transaction Costs

The larger and more elaborate the deal, the more time, energy, and money in such things as professional fees, travel, and phone charges you'll spend closing it.

Also, deals made in one area may demand further spending in others. For instance, a company buys needed machinery at the right price but must then install it, retool other equipment, and adjust its assembly line. You may not consider this a pure transaction cost, but it's another expense, nonetheless.

What the Other Side Wants

Finally, there is the most obvious downside of all: what the other side is asking you to give them. I save this for last because now that we've explored all the factors, you can reverse figure 1.3, applying it as if you were in the other side's shoes. Not only will this help you better understand a deal's true value, but it will help you better understand your opponent, increasing your effectiveness when you later have to negotiate.

Evaluating Value

Evaluating a deal is a continuing process that'll go on right up to and even past the moment you sign on the dotted line. When you negotiate, return to this section to create arguments for and against your price or your terms and conditions. For additional perspectives, see figure 1.5. By stressing the pros and cons of *not* doing the deal, it presents the flip side of this inquiry.

THE UPSIDE AND DOWNSIDE OF *NOT* DOING A DEAL		
	Upside	Downside
Not doing the deal	Avoid risks Can do other deals Save transaction costs Don't have to trade what you have	Forgo benefits • dollar value • long-term potential • subjective value

Fig. 1.5

ALTERNATIVES: HOW TO BE A BUSINESS GENIUS

If your mind is empty, it is always ready for anything; it is open to everything. In the beginner's mind there are many possibilities; in the expert's mind there are few.
—Shunryu Suzuki, *Zen Mind, Beginner's Mind*

The business world thrives on vigorous innovation. Everything our modern economy offers—from computers, telecommunications, and fast food to biotechnology, financial derivatives, and a never-ending array of consumer goods—supports the notion that business is all about creativity. Yet, though businesspeople foster originality in marketing, management, and product development, they often overlook the creative side of deal making. But why? After all, before you commit to a deal, shouldn't you consider *all* your alternatives?

Believe it or not, business creativity, to a large degree, can be taught (see figure 1.6). Below are some of the best ways for deal makers to nurture their ingenuity. These techniques will solve problems, increase your negotiating power by giving you alternatives, boost your self-confidence, and help you make better deals for more money with less risk. Besides, they're also a lot of fun. So for the next few pages forget the negative self-talk: "They'll laugh at me for even suggesting it." "We've always done it that way." "Oh, I'm just not very creative." Keep your mind open and your attitude positive. Remember, when it comes to being a creative person, you are if you think you are.

10 WAYS TO BECOME A MORE CREATIVE PERSON

1. *Change your routine.* Alter your schedule, your diet, your exercise, your entertainment, and how you get from one place to another.

2. *Read widely.* Try books, magazines, and periodicals you ordinarily wouldn't. Biographies, how-to books, and other nonfiction are especially helpful.

3. *Be curious.* Think. Notice things. Did you know that the roll-on deodorant applicator was developed from the ballpoint pen? Constantly ask "Why?" and "Why not?"

4. *Travel.* Broaden your horizons by seeing the world.

5. *Check out different TV shows and radio stations.* Millions of people enjoy programs you never even consider watching. See how the other half lives, and you'll see things in a new way. If you have an opinion, learn the other side's arguments.

6. *Keep learning.* Stretch your mind. If you're used to making deals in one business, learn how deals are made in another. Understand, compare, and adapt what's useful.

7. *Write down your ideas.* Insights can be delicate and fleeting. Capture them. Carry a notepad or tape recorder wherever you go.

8. *Set an idea quota.* This was one of Thomas Edison's favorites. He aimed at one minor invention every ten days, and one major one every six months.

9. *Go on-line.* In cyberspace you can eavesdrop or interact with people you'd never meet in real life. It's a powerful way to broaden your perspective.

10. *Talk to everyone.* You can learn from everyone, and sometimes the nonexpert has the best perspective of all. Just before the 1929 crash Joseph Kennedy took the advice of a bootblack and pulled out of the stock market.

Fig. 1.6

Look at the Big Picture

On pages 5–9 we already considered the ultimate big-picture question: "Why am I doing this deal?" Pinpoint the answer, and better ways to get what you want will often jump right out at you. At other times, all it takes is the willingness to ask yourself if there are alternatives. Whole new worlds will open up. The magic words are: "How else?"

For example, an unsophisticated inventor assumes that his only option is to sell a brilliant new idea outright to some megacorporation for a pittance of a royalty. By considering how else he could make a profit, he suddenly realizes he could also: (1) approach competitors of that company; (2) find a smaller partner who'll offer better terms; (3) wait until he has an irresistible working prototype so he can cut a better deal; (4) license just part of the idea; (5) take on a second job and finance his own manufacturing and distribution; or (6) call an expert such as a patent lawyer for help.

Look at the Little Picture

Just as you can be more general, you can also be more specific. To examine a deal in more detail, try this little ditty from Rudyard Kipling: "I keep six honest serving men/(They taught me all I knew);/ Their names are What and Why and When/And How and Where and Who." Let's say you're a business owner with a space problem who thinks the only solution is to make a deal to lease or buy a larger facility. Instead, you may ask yourself:

What is taking up so much space?

Why should I keep everything?

When can I do this?

How can I make more room?

Where else can I put everything?

Who can help me?

Considering these questions might generate the following options: Throw out whatever is not needed, have a garage sale, give unneeded items to charity and take a tax deduction, add a second story or additional room to the existing space, rent additional off-site storage, hire a professional organizer. Depending on your circumstances, any one of these may be a better solution than moving.

Brainstorming

Although this term has become synonymous with creative thinking generally, it's actually a distinct technique with specific rules. A carefully selected group gathers in a relaxed setting. A leader and a recorder are chosen. Then everybody throws out ideas with one proviso: No criticism is allowed. Criticism inhibits the creative process. The goal is to create an uninhibited environment in which to generate as many unique and even wild ideas as possible. Later, the group can select and work with the best. Of course, you can do this on your own. Just open your mind and write down everything that surfaces the instant it comes to mind. You never know which outrageous idea will lead to the really brilliant one.

Diagramming

Think of this as visual free association minus the couch and the analyst. Start by writing your basic problem in the center of a blank piece of paper. Then let your imagination do the rest. Check out figure 1.7. See how one idea almost magically leads to the next.

Scamper

If you learn only one technique, this may be the best. Credit goes to Alex Osborn, one of the original creativity teachers, who first developed it, and to Bob Eberle, who put it as follows:

S	Substitute
C	Combine
A	Adapt
M	Magnify
P	Put to Other Uses
E	Eliminate or Minimize
R	Reverse

MAPPING OUT ALTERNATIVES

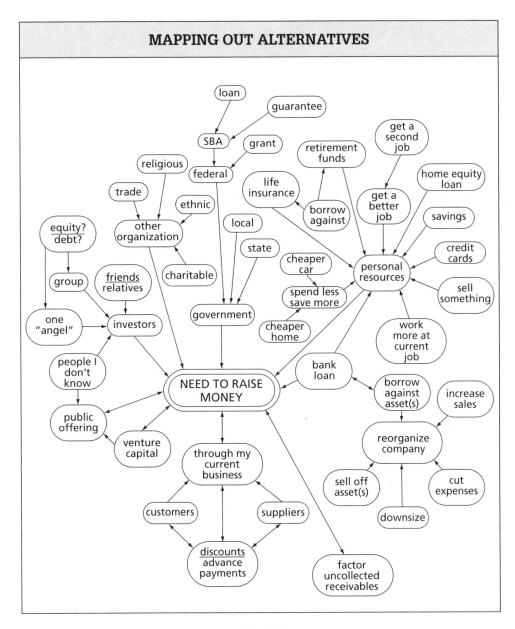

Fig. 1.7

Examine different aspects of your deal. You can use the six honest serving men: What, Why, When, How, Where, and Who (see page 17) to help you divide things up. Then take each one and run the SCAMPER checklist. Sometimes all you need is one great idea to make a career, a fortune, or both. Here are some real-life success stories that illustrate how this might work:

Substitute

When Frances Xavier McNamara dreamed up the first multipurpose credit card in the 1950s, the Diners Club card, it was based on a simple substitution: "Why pay now, when you can pay later?" When lending governments swap debt for equity, when labor negotiators switch personnel, when employees bargain for fringe benefits instead of salary, they are all using the principle of substitution.

Combine

In business, two companies may join forces to acquire a third. Film producers attach elements (a director or stars) to get their projects "green-lighted" by a studio. Real estate developers court "anchor" tenants such as major chains and department stores to secure financing.

Adapt

Applying a few basics from corporate finance, artist, professor, and iconoclast Robert Cenedella sold shares in his vibrant painting of the New York Stock Exchange, *2001: A Stock Odyssey*. In real estate, players slap liens on property to ensure loan repayments. In the film business, studios place liens on unproduced screenplays to recoup their development costs should their projects later end up with a competitor. Turn to pages 94–95 and figure 4.4 to see some ways the concept of insurance has been adapted to protect the deal maker. Don't let traditional business practices in your field fence you in. Many times a commonly used device in one area can work equally well in another.

Magnify

Think more. An investment bank "soft dollars" one deal into two: It reduces its profits on the first deal if its customer will let the bank make it up on the second. Think longer. A manufacturer negotiates to extend the term of a favorable output deal or lease. Think bigger. Lee Iacocca looks not to the private sector but to the federal government for the $1.2 billion debt guarantee to jump-start Chrysler.

Put to Other Uses
Michael Milken didn't invent junk bonds, but he was the first to use them to finance corporate takeovers. Lewis Ranieri, Steve Joseph, and Bob Dall of Salomon Brothers didn't invent residential mortgages, but they were the first to package and sell them as securities, creating the GNMA bond market.

Eliminate or Minimize
What can you leave out? The uniform price policies of big companies eliminate negotiation. Agreements to leave certain items to future good-faith negotiation save time and build relationships. Also ask yourself if you should do less of a deal. Can you lease instead of buy? Do one year instead of two? Divide your deal into steps?

Reverse
Henry Ford's creation of the assembly line was a classic reversal: Rather than having workers travel to the work, he had the work travel to the workers. To reduce accidents caused by older train engineers, American Express created the first pension plan, in effect paying them not to work! The sale-leaseback is a classic way for real estate owners to raise quick cash while continuing to enjoy their property.

Some Other Creativity Exercises

Here are a few other neat tricks:

Reversing Nouns and Verbs
Instead of lending to the partners, can you partner with the lender? Instead of exporting for the manufacturer, can you manufacture for the exporter? This is a lot like the reversal from SCAMPER.

Crystal Ball
What economic, technological, political, or personal forces affect your deal? Can you develop a few alternate scenarios based on their interplay? How would you react to each one?

Devil's Advocate
Can you think of and evaluate every single reason why your deal is lousy, risky, or just plain not worth doing? Once you've divided the obstacles into discrete pieces, overcoming them may be easier than you think.

The Wheel of Deals

As you know, the six steps of the Deal Power System are Step Back, Get Help, Check Things Out, Minimize Risk, Negotiate, and Write It Down. Mix and match them. What would it be like to *negotiate* how you'll *check things out*? To *step back* and think about how you'll *write things down*? To *get help minimizing risk*? In some ways this is the most potent technique of all!

Intuition and Creativity

"The final act of business judgment is intuitive," said the legendary Alfred P. Sloane, former president of General Motors. Up to this point, we've focused on rational and analytical ways to jump-start creativity. But what about those brilliant and spontaneous flashes of insight? Where do they come from? And how can we have more of them?

The Proverbial Lightbulb

We live in a scientific age that tends to devalue intuition. To some degree we all have intuition; we just tend to ignore it. When Conrad Hilton was bidding for the Stevens Hotel in Chicago, a number popped into his head. He put that number on the table and bought the world's largest hotel for just $200 more than the next best offer! Start tuning in to your inner voice and feelings. Just because you can't explain your hunches and gut feelings doesn't mean you shouldn't profit from them.

Relaxation

"No man can think clearly when his fists are clenched," said drama critic George Jean Nathan. Intuition works best when you're relaxed. Define your problem, study it, and then forget about it for a while. Do something that really calms you down, and let your subconscious take over. After the government changed money-market deposit regulations, Wayne Silby, founder of the Calvert Group, cooked up a brilliant $800 million program that would allow him to work with, instead of against, the banks; it all came to him while relaxing in a floatation tank. Your breakthrough idea may come when you least expect it.

Dreams

Descartes's philosophy, Robert Louis Stevenson's novels, Einstein's theory of relativity, Michael Jackson's music, Elias Howe's sewing machine, Mendeleyev's periodic table, Samuel Taylor Coleridge's "Kubla Khan," and Jack Nicklaus's golf grip all came out of dreams.

Guides

Socrates had a spirit guide, or *daemon*. General Douglas MacArthur used to discuss military strategy with an imaginary hero-father figure. Do you have any business or personal heroes? If not, conjure one up. Ask yourself: What would they do in your shoes? Consider this from James M. Benham, founder and chairman of the Capital Preservation Fund: "Whenever I have heavy problems I simply introduce the question to my mind . . . and in time, I always get an answer. . . . I think I have spiritual friends. I believe they will have me pick up a book or a magazine or read something somewhere, or have someone say something to me to give me input to help me with questions that I have to deal with. . . . That's how strange it is with me."

Poking Your Gut

And if your subconscious doesn't throw you pearls on a regular basis, here are a couple of ways to encourage it:

Toss a coin. Ask yourself how you feel about the outcome. Why?

Scribble. This was one of Leonardo da Vinci's favorites. Go crazy. What do you get?

Force comparison. Open the dictionary and pick a word at random. How is your problem like an apple, a porcupine, or an umbrella?

Write with your nondominant hand. Many psychologists think it helps access the more creative and intuitive childlike part of your personality.

Ask an object. Relax and close your eyes. Think of your question. Then open your eyes. Let the first object you look at talk to you and tell you the answer.

Simplicity

Approaching your deals creatively has a few drawbacks; developing and contemplating alternatives takes time. If you come up bone-dry, your only solace may be a self-proclaimed A for effort. Also, you risk making things too complicated. In most businesses, there are good reasons for the standard ways that deals are done. Everybody understands them and, basically, they work. Do something new or fancy and you can count on more time explaining, documenting, and administering your brainchild. So keep your mind open, but before you abandon the tried and true, make sure it's worth it!

THE BIRD'S-EYE VIEW

> If you don't do your homework, you won't
> make your free throws.
>
> —Larry Bird

Now you have some great tools to set goals, estimate value, and create alternatives. In short, here is a quick way to get a panoramic view of any deal. If Socrates were in business today, I'm sure he'd proclaim, "The unexamined deal is not worth doing."

2

STEP 2:

GET HELP

Here lies a man who knew how to enlist into
his service better men than himself.
—Andrew Carnegie's epitaph

Given the complexities of modern business, only a foolish deal maker flies solo. Sure, some big shots enjoy the spotlight, but the credit is never theirs alone. For example, great industrialists, like Ron Perelman, work with a veritable dream team of advisers. Of course, few of us mere mortals barter in Fortune 500 companies, but whatever your level, you've got to get good people in your corner.

In this step we survey the expert help available to the deal maker. In Chapter 8 we'll detail how to hire them. Some professionals, like lawyers and accountants, play a part in most deals, while others, like appraisers and specialized consultants, assist only in particular ones. Regardless, every deal maker should be aware of the resources on which they might draw. For woe to those who should have asked, but didn't!

LAWYERS

I wouldn't write a song about any of them.
—John Lennon

Forget all the lawyer jokes. If you're making any kind of sizable deal, you'll need at least one attorney on your side. And while my brothers and sisters at the bar may have a reputation for being arrogant, pushy, callous, and sneaky, I guarantee you'll be far more forgiving when you've got a sharp one working for you. Because of their skill at navigating the ever expanding legal universe and their intimate knowledge of contract law—in essence, the law of deals—they're an invaluable ally for any deal maker.

How Lawyers Help Deal Makers

Many people think that all lawyers earn their living in court trying cases. Not true. Transactional lawyers specialize in making deals, usually in a chosen area of expertise. They're the people to ask when you need:

• *Help complying with the law.* As Mark Twain said, "If you laid all of our laws end to end, there would be no end." The more complex the deal, the more laws exist that affect it. Solid advice on tax, securities, labor, real estate, corporate matters, intellectual property (patents, trademarks, and copyrights), antitrust or environmental law may be vital to your deal. Like doctors, lawyers specialize.

• *Due diligence.* Legal due diligence, which is, among other things, a thorough assessment of the other side's ownership rights, capacity, and authority, is a transactional attorney's bread and butter. More about this in Step 3 on pages 73–79.

• *Cogent business advice.* As law students, attorneys learned to sift through facts and isolate key issues, a form of analysis that is enormously helpful to the businessperson. Also, years of doing deals in a particular area imparts much practical wisdom. Prevent false starts by getting your lawyer in the loop early.

• *A negotiator.* Lawyers constantly negotiate. A good one knows all the arguments, industry standards, and tricks of the trade. Because everybody expects them to be difficult, they make great foils or buffers. Since they're so involved in all the details leading up to closing, they can be excellent at coordinating everyone's efforts.

• *Formal paperwork.* Attorneys are experts at drafting contracts, contracts that can give you a big leg up down the road. See Step 6 on pages 154–58 and Step 4 at pages 100–107. Also, the files your lawyer keeps while doing your deal may be key if you need to litigate.

• *Broker: mover and shaker.* Some transactional lawyers are powerful players in their own right, gaining you instant credibility. With their golden network, they may find you money or make a key introduction.

• *A litigator.* If all else fails, you can always sue. Just remember that most transactional lawyers don't litigate. For this you'll need a "wartime consigliere." More about this on pages 212–13.

Deal Breaker or Deal Maker?

I feel sorry for anyone shopping for their first lawyer. It's always tough for a member of the laity to evaluate the integrity and competence of the expert they wish to rely upon. This is especially true of the lawyer, whose language and work product are particularly "user-unfriendly."

So, the layperson does the usual: They get recommendations from others in their business community; they seek out and call various referral services; they check the Yellow Pages and legal directories like *Martindale-Hubbell*, *Who's Who in American Law*, or *The Best Lawyers in America*; they contact the state bar to check licensing, educational background, and disciplinary records; and they even (I hope) try to pick a specialist with the right temperament: a diligent draftsmen to iron out details, a diplomat to massage a cranky opponent, or a hard-charger to rape and pillage for them. All this is good, but here's one special warning:

Get a deal maker, not a deal breaker! This is a clichéd but decisive distinction. Because they're trained to tie up every loose end, lawyers can be too slow. Because they're worried about malpractice, they can be too thorough. Because they're scared of other lawyers stealing their clients, they can try too hard. Because they're taught to be adversarial, they can alienate people. Because they often bill by the hour, they may drag deals out to make more money.

So, get a deal maker from the start—someone who never loses sight of the big picture. And control your attorney. When documents are too fat, remote issues too many, negotiations inexplicably testy, and explanations too flimsy, chances are you've got a deal breaker on your payroll. Don't let any attorney "What if?" your deal to death with fantastic contingencies that would baffle even a bar examiner. Remember, when it comes to deciding how much risk to take, you have the last word.

Legal Ethics

The term is not an oxymoron. Lawyers are much more concerned with ethical behavior than you might think. Technically, they're officers of the court; their actions are governed by case law and laws like the Model Rules of Professional Conduct. In California, for example, 80 percent of the bar dues collected (around $40 million per year) are spent disciplining attorneys. Lawyers know (and you should know) that if they screw up badly enough they may be reprimanded, placed on probation, suspended, disbarred, and/or sued for malpractice. Thus, among other things, expect your attorney to represent you competently and zealously, to disclose all actual and potential conflicts of interest, to keep all of your communications confidential, and to maintain a separate trust account for any monies he or she might hold for you.

ACCOUNTANTS

> MAX BIALISTOCK: Who's gonna find out? It's only $2,000. Bloom, do me a favor. Move a few decimal points around. You can do it. You're an accountant. You're in a noble profession. The word "Count" is part of your title.
>
> —Mel Brooks, *The Producers*

The Profession: A Quick Overview

The AICPA (American Institute of Certified Public Accountants) and the FASB (Financial Accounting Standards Board) establish standards (like GAAP—generally accepted accounting principles) and speak for the profession. The certified public accountant (CPA) is the designation of choice; a national uniform exam, state licensing requirements, continuing education, and so on are required. Like law firms, accounting firms come in all shapes and sizes, from the international "Big Six" (Arthur Andersen, Coopers & Lybrand, Deloitte & Touche, Ernst & Young, KPMG Peat Marwick, and Price Waterhouse) to nationals, mininationals, regionals, locals, and sole practitioners. The AICPA runs a peer-review program for participating firms that may help you to make your selection.

The Accountant and the Deal Maker

Mostly, accountants monitor the financial pulse of an organization: watching accounts payable and receivable, tracking inventory, anticipating cash flow, putting together financials and other records, troubleshooting, ferreting out fraud, and the like. Upper-echelon accountants are an integral part of management. When deals are made they can be indispensable for:

- *Financial advice.* An accountant can help analyze, create, find, and choose among opportunities. They can often tell whether a project is feasible. They can prepare financial projections to attract investors.
- *Pricing a deal.* Though their focus is more numerical and less strategic than investment bankers (discussed below), accountants are key to finding the bottom line.
- *Tax advice.* Every deal has tax consequences; an accountant can help minimize what you'll owe.
- *Due diligence.* Financial statements can be deceptive. See the section entitled "Cooking the Books" on pages 54–63. On the flip side, a keen CPA may uncover opportunities, such as steeply undervalued assets, that the other side may be unaware of. Accountants also certify statements for lenders or investors.
- *Prepping the books.* Sometimes, for example, in order to comfort investors or hook a buyer, you want your business to show big profits; sometimes, particularly at tax time, you don't. When possible, plan this years in advance.
- *Auditing.* When one side must give up a slice of the profits by way of ongoing payments, the other may need an accountant to make sure they get their fair share.
- *Management consulting.* Firms may offer efficiency studies, computer expertise, executive recruiting, litigation, statistical and actuarial support, and even psychological business counseling.

The Three Basic Financial Statement Services

Whether you're buying, selling, investing, or lending, objective information about a company's financial health is essential. Basically, there are three choices when it comes to financial statements.

The Audit

The audit is the top-of-the-line service: an independent accountant's examination of a company's financials leading (hopefully) to an unqualified formal written opinion that they fairly show that company's financial position under GAAP. In performing one, a CPA will break down, compare, and recompute accounts; trace entries by examining supporting documents like invoices and canceled checks; confirm transactions with third parties; perform physical inspections; do analytical reviews (for instance, comparing current information with that from prior years, or against the industry, or with nonfinancial data); question unusual fluctuations; and so on. Large accounting firms encourage their clients to choose an audit because it's the best and most expensive service they offer. Annual audits are mandatory for public companies.

The Statement on Auditing Standards 53 and 54 states that audits should "provide reasonable assurance of detecting errors and irregularities that are material to the financial statements . . . but [generally do] not include procedures specifically designed to detect illegal acts." Thus, as good as an audit can be, it is not an ironclad guarantee. For one thing, a typical audit isn't a detailed or complete one (which verifies every single transaction); instead, accounts are reviewed on a test basis (i.e., through statistical sampling). Also, as we'll see in Step 3, GAAP can be used to mislead and conceal. For example, Chrysler's 1980 audited financials gave little warning of impending insolvency. Finally, audits rely heavily on a company's internal controls, the integrity of its management, and the skill, judgment, and honesty of the auditor. As we know from scandals like Equity Funding, ZZZZ Best, and the S and L crisis, compromise one or more of these and you compromise the audit. Still, remember: The audit is your best bet by far and you should be wary of relying on anything else.

The Review

After a successful review the most a CPA can say in a formal written opinion is that they're "not aware of any material changes required to conform the financial statements with GAAP." This is a far cry from the audit. Reviews are based on inquiries of a company's personnel. Standards 53 and 54 (see above) don't apply, and far less emphasis is placed on such things as understanding internal policies, testing records, and corroborating evidence.

Small accounting firms often prefer reviews to audits. It's less exposure for them, and they often lack the clout to sell their client on an audit. But is a review really a good substitute? Maybe, but only if the examined company maintains great records, you keep in mind its limitations, and you know the industry well enough to know what to look for.

The Compilation

The compilation is the least reliable method. A company supplies data and the CPA simply compiles it into a set of statements. Accountants like the compilation: No inquiries or opinions are required, and that usually means easy money for the CPA. A compilation may be the right choice for a company that's either extraordinarily well run, can't afford better, or just doesn't want a CPA snooping around—in which case, be forewarned.

Opinions and the "Creative" Accountant

As you read "Cooking the Books" on pages 54–63, you'll quickly realize that CPAs have quite a bit of poetic license when it comes to prepping financials. Naturally, when you hire someone to do your books, you want a CPA who can arrange the numbers as attractively as possible. However, both the Securities and Exchange Commission and the profession prohibit opinion shopping. Here, you'll need a little extra savvy.

With an audit, anything less than a *clean* or *unqualified* opinion (for example, a *qualified opinion* or a *disclaimer* of an opinion) can only hurt a company. (See fig. 3.2 on page 56.) Piecemeal opinions aren't allowed because they're considered misleading, and no CPA wants to issue an adverse opinion and risk losing a client. Obviously, the CPA who has uncovered some dirt on his or her client is in an odd position . . . and we can only imagine what goes on behind closed doors. Thus, expect your CPA to do everything they can to help you paint a rosy picture, provided that they: (1) can justify their choices under GAAP; (2) can honor their legal duty to make full and fair disclosure; and (3) don't end up in jail. Also, to uphold applicable ethical standards, an accountant must be free from even the appearance of bias. Although this is probably more important when you're evaluating the other side's CPA, you don't want them questioning your choice, either.

INVESTMENT BANKERS

> The bigger the bankroll, the tighter
> the rubber band.
>
> —Anonymous

In the deal-making jungle, investment banks are the kings of beasts, powerful institutions that help other powerful institutions wheel and deal. Because they play with millions, even billions of dollars, few of us will ever be in a position to hire a Morgan Stanley, First Boston, or Goldman, Sachs. Even so, every deal maker has much to learn from their blend of creativity, assertiveness, and street smarts.

What Investment Banks Do

Uniquely American, investment banks (I.B.s) became prominent as middlemen for European capital invested in the great boom of the late 1800s. Today, I.B.s wear many hats and thus make money every which way:

• *Adviser/Strategist/Broker.* I.B.s help clients figure out their long- and short-term goals. They are business enzymes. Because of their place in the deal stream, they can easily alert companies to existing opportunities and broker or brainstorm new ones. They can counsel either the acquiring or the acquired and help restructure financing, balance sheets, tax liabilities, and bankruptcies. They assist privately held companies when they go public (issue stock) and publicly held companies when they go private (buy that stock back). Through their knowledge and connections I.B.s often add value to a deal.

• *Agent/"Hired Gun."* No matter how companies are introduced, when they marry, divorce, or die or beget, adopt, or disown children, I.B.s will analyze, structure, negotiate, and, in short, make the deal on their behalf.

• *Underwriter.* I.B.s are best known for selling securities. This complex job entails the preparation of special disclosure documents for investors (the prospectus), due diligence, compliance with federal and state laws, formation of a syndicate to help distribute the securities, and other requirements.

• *Valuation Expert.* Tax, bankruptcy, corporate, and other laws often require a professional opinion as to how much a company and/or its assets are worth. I.B.s can provide a formal written fairness opinion, certifying a particular exchange as equitable.

• *Financier.* I.B.s often become players themselves by putting their own money into a deal.

• *Supplier of Technical Services.* Some houses can help you clear an unbelievable volume of daily stock transactions; others have research departments that virtually know it all. In running their own businesses, I.B.s develop cutting-edge technical support, especially for communications and computers. As you'd expect, they turn this overhead into profit by selling it to others.

• *Investment Manager.* Many companies have sizable portfolios of their own; I.B.s can help manage them.

The Field

Today, a dozen or so *special* or *bulge bracket* firms dominate investment banking. (Public offerings are announced with *tombstone* ads, listing key players in descending order; I.B.s fight for top billing in the special or bulge bracket as vigorously as Hollywood talent fight for their credits.) If you want to engage an I.B., know that the big ones serve huge, sophisticated companies; others serve less knowledgeable, medium or emerging ones; an I.B. may also work market niches through expertise in such areas as mergers and acquisitions *(M&A)*, noninvestment-grade bonds *(junk bonds)*, or wide-ranging distribution. I.B.s may also be categorized by the geographic area or industry they handle and, of course, by reputation. Generally, the internal pecking order goes like this: chairman, president, member of the executive (or management) committee, managing director (partner), vice president, and associate.

Relationships: Meaningful, Confidential, and Otherwise

In the old days, companies maintained long-term, monogamous relationships with their bankers. Today, they spread business among several I.B.s, the same I.B.s share customers, and time and again, companies and I.B.s work with each other in syndicates and across the table in M&A. Thus, personnel have preexisting and active relationships at all levels, requiring careful management on all sides. As you might imagine, when information flows through such an incestuous network, breached confidentiality, betrayed loyalties, and conflicts of interest, both subtle and blatant, proliferate in ever-fascinating permutations. For example: The I.B. uses sensitive information obtained from one client to advise its competitor; the I.B.'s research department issues an unflattering report about the same company that another department of the I.B. is courting; or the I.B. dumps the stock of one client from the portfolios it's managing for others. And, of course, there are always the sensational insider trading scandals. Securities and other industry laws help keep things in check, but they're far from perfect. Some I.B.s go above and beyond in trying to avoid these scenarios, setting up communication barriers between departments, or restricted and watch lists prohibiting the trading of certain stocks. Still, there are problems.

All this means that you'll need extra political acumen to handle an I.B. For one thing, check the public record (see Step 3); when it comes to large institutions like I.B.s, it'll be full of information that may reveal potential and actual conflicts of interest. Talk to people in your business network. Put other professionals on your team who can be objective about the bank because they do not have a long-standing relationship with it and are not looking for referrals. Then, talk frankly with the I.B. about any concerns you may have. Because an I.B. would probably be considered your legal *fiduciary*, it has a duty to make the best deal it can for you, to disclose all conflicts of interest and all other relevant material facts, and to hold information received from you as confidential. However, since the law isn't fully settled in this area, reminding the I.B. of these duties in a formal contract is a good preventative. Finally, watch everything you say to an I.B. For example, an innocent inquiry by a high-ranking executive about a company's value could easily spark rumors that that company is in play. Remember: There's no such thing as a secret.

Fees—the Really Big Bucks

In the world of M&A, I.B.s routinely broker deals, taking a slice of the proceeds paid or received. When Fortune 500 companies trade hands, multimillion-dollar fees are common. For example, when Texaco acquired Getty Oil in 1984, Goldman, Sachs pocketed $18.5 million! I.B.s justify these numbers by pointing to their expertise, the value they add to the deal (which greatly exceeds their fees), the fact that they could just as well rake in the dough arbitraging from the sidelines, and the risk they take because they don't get paid on deals that don't close. They also know that when big careers and big businesses are in extremis, the engagement of a top-drawer I.B. is management's insurance policy against the litigious shareholders who'll strain to second-guess them. Every deal maker can admire this kind of moxie; keep this in mind as you read the following section.

AGENTS AND BROKERS

> The dead actor had requested in his will that his body be cremated and ten percent of his ashes thrown in his agent's face.
>
> —Anonymous

Generically, a broker or an agent is a middleman who finds and/or closes a deal for someone else. In certain industries (for example, real estate, entertainment, and securities) they're licensed and their role and compensation are clearly defined by law and/or custom. However, in the business world at large, many lawyers, bankers, and others can and do act as finders, go-betweens, or matchmakers—i.e., brokers or agents—in all sorts of deals. Before you give one the green light, do the following:

• *Talk about your expectations.* Just because someone's got a law or business degree or some fancy title doesn't mean they can deliver what they promise. Check them out first.

• *Be specific about what they're brokering.* You don't want them trying to commission something they had nothing to do with.

• *Reserve final authority.* No one should be able to commit you to a deal but you. If all you've engaged them to do is to make an introduction, consider cutting off or limiting their involvement as soon as that's been done.

• *Be careful about giving anyone the exclusive right to make your deal.* Brokers strongly prefer an exclusive because it protects them from being sidestepped. But if they've got a big hat and no cows, that exclusive will keep you hog-tied when they either can't deliver or won't bother trying. And no doubt they'll be the first to yell for their cut if you go out and make a deal on your own.

• *Set a deadline.* If nothing's happened after an agreed period of time, you should have the right to cut your agent or broker loose, no strings attached. This is especially true when they've had you on an exclusive.

• *Define the percentage.* See pages 199–200. There's more to consider here than just a simple number.

PRIVATE INVESTIGATORS

> I keep two magnums in my desk. One's a gun and I keep it loaded. The other's a bottle and it keeps *me* loaded.
>
> —Bill Watterson, "Calvin and Hobbes"

In my experience, it's amazing how rarely hiring a detective is even considered. Yet when key players are total strangers and there's big money and big risk, how can you afford not to? Maybe all the media caricatures make it impossible for businesspeople to take them seriously. Or maybe private eyes are too secretive to market themselves effectively. Anyway, the average deal maker would sooner spend $25,000 to have their lawyer prepare the perfect contract than $1,000 to find out whether the other side is dirt poor or crooked.

What Your Gumshoe Can Do for You

Although detectives can do many things, like find missing persons, arrange electronic surveillance and countersurveillance, bodyguard, perform handwriting analysis, and administer polygraph tests, what a deal maker really needs up front is a background check on the character and competence of the other side and/or intelligence that will provide an edge in negotiation.

It's not nearly as clandestine as you might think. There is an unbelievable amount of data on the information highway, especially public records. Today's cyber-sleuth knows how to get it, sift it, cross-check it, digest it, and make sense of it. Of course, they can always make the rounds by phone or by foot as well. We'll get a lot more specific about how and what they find on pages 63–73 in Step 3: Check It Out.

If you're lucky, what is dug up will be black or white: The other side's good for what they say they are, or they're a bunch of ex-cons with gambling debts, drug problems, and ties to organized crime. However, be prepared for gray areas that make you go "Hmmm . . ." For instance, Mr. "Straight Shooter" is defending an unusual number of lawsuits. Or that seemingly rock-solid board of directors is actually deeply divided about the deal.

Selecting and Working with Your Shamus

Because there are no standard educational requirements and the criteria for licensing, which is mandated by over half the states in this country, vary widely, picking a winner is tough. Good word of mouth and a good gut feeling about your candidate are both crucial. It takes certain personality traits to excel at detective work: skepticism, resourcefulness, and a knack for getting people to talk. Thus, a sly high-school dropout with the right touch might outshine an ex-CIA (or FBI or KGB) agent with a wall full of weird certificates. You'll get your best referrals from other professionals who've done business with a particular P.I. Also consider the following:

• *Is it worth it?* Basically this depends on the stakes. Reframe the question: "Will what you find or don't find be worth the detective's fee?"

• *Private eyes come in all shapes and sizes.* Distinguish the private investigator, who may serve up all sorts of "detective" type services (see above), from the *information broker*, who's more research oriented and often has a degree in library science, from the *public records researcher*, who does just that. Kroll Associates in New York (212-593-1000) is the Rolls-Royce of investigative firms. They've been hired by the Kuwaiti government to find Saddam Hussein's hidden assets, the Port Authority to revamp security after the World Trade Center bombing, and hundreds of major domestic and multinational companies to verify assets, aid in battles for corporate control, and perform background checks on potential partners. CDB Infotek (800-555-3513) offers "do-it-yourself" on-line access to hundreds of public record databases (for example, Litigation Histories, Real Property, Aircraft and Vehicle Ownership, Tax Records, Bankruptcies). The Resource Line (800-338-3463) can refer you to over 8,500 detective agencies. After the work is completed, clients are asked to evaluate the agency they hired; although that information is not available to prospective clients, it is used to determine whether the Resource Line will continue to make a particular referral. For those doing business abroad, the Information Professionals Network (415-364-6121) is an international network of due diligence professionals, private and financial fraud investigators, and business intelligence researchers. Also consider the American Society for Industrial Security (703-522-5800), the National Association of Certified Fraud Examiners (800-872-4678), and the National Association of Investigative Specialists (512-420-9292). Regardless of who you hire, hourly, daily, or flat fees are the norm; rates vary widely.

• *Get a "white hat" investigator.* By ignoring laws relating to stalking, harassment, slander, or invasion of privacy, an overly zealous operative can get you in big trouble. For instance, statutes regarding the taping of telephone calls vary widely from state to state. Your P.I. should know these and other pertinent laws cold.

• *Work in stages.* For example, before you do a national search, start with the counties or states where your target is most likely to be doing, or have done, business. Get a written report. Then decide whether to expand the investigation. Not only will this save time and money, it'll let you try out your Sam Spade on smaller jobs before you make a large commitment.

APPRAISERS

CECIL GRAHAM: What is a cynic?
LORD DARLINGTON: A man who knows the price of every-
thing and the value of nothing.
—Oscar Wilde, *Lady Windermere's Fan*

"How much?" is the question appraisers earn their living answering. Though their job may overlap with investment bankers' and accountants', the appraiser is really the specialist at pricing just about anything: going concerns, real estate, machinery, jewelry, gems, collectibles, fine art, and so on.

Unlike accountants, bankers, or lawyers, appraisers generally are not regulated by state or federal law; real estate appraisers are the exception. Thus, educational background, certifications, and titles vary widely. Prominent organizations include the American Society of Appraisers (which can refer you to someone local), the Appraisers Association of America (good for fine arts), the International Society of Appraisers, and the National Society of Real Estate Appraisers. Always make sure the appraiser specializes in the item you'd like appraised.

Appraisals work best when limited to particular items or issues. Don't give an appraisal too much weight. As we know from Step 1, the value of a deal is a complex, and to some extent subjective, question. Only you know what a deal is really worth to you.

Get a Sample

One unique thing about hiring an appraiser is that it's O.K. to ask for a sample of his or her work: a past appraisal. Above all, a good appraisal should be thorough, so look for:

1. A complete and precise description of what's being appraised.
2. Some indication of why the appraisal is being requested (for example, tax, insurance, sale).
3. All information, data, backup, methods, and formulas used to arrive at the appraised value.
4. The appraised value.
5. Any special qualifications or conditions to the appraised value.
6. The appraiser's signature and certification.

Hiring

Never hire an appraiser whose fee is based on the appraised value; such an arrangement can only jeopardize their objectivity. Be clear about who the appraiser is working for, as shared accountability can also compromise their judgment. Of course, if the other side is the one hiring the appraiser, make sure you understand and agree with all the assumptions and methods their appraiser uses.

An hourly rate is the way to go, and if the job takes longer than you'd expect, don't be surprised. Research and authentication, if required, take time. You can request a preliminary opinion before authorizing a full appraisal. Usually, it's better to bring in an appraiser early, before either side fixes on a price. However, if the other side is likely to look at your appraiser's price as your first offer, make sure you get to review that appraisal before it's delivered; otherwise you may be put in an awkward position.

CONSULTANTS

A consultant is a man who knows 146 ways to
make love but doesn't know any women.

—Anonymous

For our purposes, a consultant is really a catchall, an expert who doesn't fit into a prefab professional pigeonhole. If you can name a field, from airport engineering to zoo management, someone's out there consulting in it. When a deal requires unique technical or business know-how, these specialists can really help by running studies, assisting in due diligence, monitoring compliance, giving second opinions, and so on. In certain areas, such as capital acquisition by way of accounts receivable, factoring, or private placements, consultants may even broker deals in their own right.

Finding a Consultant

The more unusual the expertise, the more resourceful you'll have to be. Network. Locate leading authorities. Check the directories: *Consultants and Consulting Organizations Directory, The Directory of Management Consultants, Dun's Consultants Directory, Experts Contact Directory,* or *National Trade and Professional Associations of the U.S.* Look at the journals in the applicable area of expertise: You can read the ads, write your own, submit a news release, or ask an editor for a referral. Also try calling the Association of Management Consulting Firms (212-697-8262).

Interviewing

It's customary for consultants to submit bids and/or detailed written proposals to get work. So go ahead and ask questions, explore different approaches, and demand explanations. They should be used to it. Through what's said and what's sent you'll know whether they're on top of your problem, what they'd do, and how long it should take to fix it. Here are some other tips:

• *Let them know what's secret.* Have them sign a confidentiality agreement. See page 129. Secrecy should start from the first moment of contact and continue for an appropriate period of time *after* the job is done.

• *Encourage their creativity.* Let them challenge assumptions, catch-phrases, and stale ways of thinking. If you want a fresh solution, don't insist on defining the problem your way.

• *Choose quality over price.* This truism applies across the board but is especially true because a consultant's services can be so unique. No consultant may be better than a mediocre one, since wasting time with the wrong one can leave you unreceptive to hiring the right one later on.

• *Set realistic deadlines.* Many consultants work part-time. Do you need their complete and undivided attention? Or can you accommodate their schedule?

• *Know whether you want more than advice.* One way to group consultants is by whether they're *advisory* or *operational.* The former will tell you what to do; the latter will help you do it.

• *Be clear about ownership.* On your nickel, a consultant may develop new ideas, compile data, create physical models, or come up with research notions that don't pan out. Negotiate for exclusive ownership of everything they create and provide for you. After all, you paid for it. If not, try for nonexclusive ownership, preferably with a hold-back period during which the consultant can't use them but you can.

SELF-HELP

The best helping hand I ever got was
at the end of my own arm.

—Anonymous

If you can't afford professional help, if it's not readily available in your industry or geographic area, or if you're doing a small deal and think it's not worth hiring it, don't despair. Reliable free advice is often just a phone call or bus ride away.

• *GO to the Library.* You'd be surprised at how much helpful information is available to you, the deal maker, at your public library. Start by asking the librarian to point you in the right direction. It's their job, and they'll save you hours. If what you want is not in, reserve it. Today, card catalogs and magazine and periodical indices can be thoroughly searched just by typing a few words in at a computer terminal. Don't forget university libraries. See figure 2.1 for some reference resources I bet you didn't know exist.

- *GO to the bookstore.* Mark Twain once said, "The man who does not read good books has no advantage over the man who can't read them." Browse. If you can't find a whole book that's on target, find another with a good chapter on your subject. Today's national bookstore chains will be more current than your library.
- *GO to the newsstand.* The right article might give you concise and invaluable insight.
- *FIND someone who's been there.* A helpful soul who's already done that deal can put you way ahead of the game.
- *GO on-line.* There are electronic bulletin boards, mailing lists, and Web pages that cater to every possible special interest. Avoid cyber-space and you're sure to become a deal-making dinosaur.
- *NETWORK.* If you don't schmooze, you lose. Find the right room, and work it.
- *CHECK your Rolodex.* Make a call. Set up lunch. Why is this often the last place we look?!
- *CHECK the Yellow Pages.* Is there a consumer or trade organization that offers free advice? An inventor- or other business-support group?
- *FIND a student.* Law schools have legal-aid clinics. Business schools run internship programs. A student is not a professional, but if you're looking for free or low-cost counseling, try one.
- *GO shopping.* Ask the right questions, and you may learn a lot from a gabby businessperson or sales rep. Try drawing them out with these kinds of questions: "I'm kind of new at this, why is what you're offering so much better?" "If I went to your competitor, what would they tell me?" "Off the record, what would you do if you were me?" You may get the party line, or you may get the real inside scoop.
- *CALL Uncle Sam.* Work the phone. Is there somebody at a federal, state, city, or local government agency that can help? See figure 2.2.

Remember: Although self-help often works out fine, it is no substitute for good professional advice. There's always a risk that your homemade approach, even when it seems like the only practical choice, will end up costing you more in the end.

YOUR MOST VALUABLE PLAYER

Behind an able man, there are always
other able men.

—Chinese proverb

You can study every on-line, in print, government, educational, and trade resource. You can hire a Noah's ark of professionals: two of every species. You can run your checklists over and over and over again. Yet, be it a spouse, a best friend, or a trusted colleague, *there's no substitute for the advice of those who know you best.*

My friend Joe is a high-ranking business-affairs executive at one of the big studios. A natural deal maker, he's savvy and real smart, with a natural charm that soft-pedals a tough demeanor. He makes his living negotiating million-dollar deals with Hollywood's finest.

Joe was buying a new home from an owner who had declared bankruptcy and, for whatever reason, this was one deal he could not close. Though ambivalent, he offered the asking price. But inspections found problems. The deal stalled. There was talk of other bidders. The bank started squawking about foreclosure. The owner became evasive about repairs. Joe's real estate agent was leaning on him for a quick sale. And in the middle of it all, Joe was waffling, uncharacteristically indecisive about the price, the property, and his priorities.

A longtime colleague took Joe aside. "Hey, what's with you? You have a reputation for playing the hard line. The company loves you for it. Besides, you gamble on everything. Since when do you balk at making a take-it-or-leave-it offer? Snap out of it." Joe promptly closed the deal, but not before knocking $65,000 off the price!

So, talk to your friends at work and at play, talk to your significant other, even if they don't know all the dirty details. Could the most expensive professional in the world have matched the insight of Joe's friend? No way.

BUSINESS REFERENCE TOOLS AT YOUR PUBLIC LIBRARY

The Burwell Directory of Information Brokers
The Directory of Directories
The Encyclopedia of Associations
National Trade and Professional Associations of the United States
Pratt's Guide to Venture Capital Resources
Books in Print
   (also: *Books in Print's Out of Print Resources* and *Forthcoming Books*)
The Index to Periodical Literature
The Encyclopedia of Business Information Sources
Gale Directory of Databases
Newsletters in Print
Dun's Regional Business Directory
Minority Organizations: A National Directory
National Directory of Women-Owned Business Firms
Thomas' Registry of American Manufacturers
The Biography Index

plus . . .

dozens of other encyclopedias, almanacs, yearbooks, databases, guides,
   manuals, directories, and handbooks . . .

Fig. 2.1

GOVERNMENT HELP FOR DEAL MAKERS

- Start with the government pages in your phone book.
- Get a copy of the *Catalog of Federal Domestic Assistance* from the U.S. Government Printing Office.
- Among other things, the Small Business Administration (SBA) offers guaranteed loans, training, advice, publications, contract assistance, and simplified business plans for the do-it-yourself entrepreneur. There are even programs for special groups, such as the Women's Network for Entrepreneurial Training (WNET) and the Minority Business Development Agency (MBDA). Call 800-8-ASK-SBA for the SBA; try 202-482-5061 for the MBDA.
- Members of the Service Corps of Retired Executives (SCORE) can give impartial advice on all types of business problems. Call 202-205-6762.
- Business Information Centers (BICs) have been set up by SCORE and the SBA in several major cities; they're business libraries for the entrepreneur with video, computer, and on-line resources available.
- The Small Business Institute (SBI) provides management counseling through faculty-supervised college students. Call 800-8-ASK-SBA.
- Small Business Development Centers (SBDC) specialize in one-on-one counseling and classroom-style training. Look for a local listing.
- ATLAS is a computerized service providing marketing and trade data for exporters. It's available through the SBA, SBI, SCORE, and SBDC.
- Through the International Trade Administration (ITA) overseen by the U.S. Department of Commerce (USDOC), U.S. exporters can access the U.S. and Foreign Commercial Service (a network of 2,500 trade experts in over sixty countries), the National Trade DataBank, the Comparison Shopping Service, and various other networking and advisory services. Not everything is free. Call 800-USA-TRAD for the USDOC and 202-482-3022 for the ITA.
- *Incubators* offer counseling to start-up companies and good deals on office space and support. Try the National Business Incubation Association at 614-593-4331.
- The Cooperative Extension Service of the Department of Agriculture can assist rural businesses. Find the local number for the Department of Agriculture or a listing for your local County Extension Office.
- Don't forget state resources. Start with the Department of Commerce.
- Don't forget local resources. Try your Chamber of Commerce.

By the way, this list is just a sample. For example, it doesn't even mention many loan programs and research-and-technology development and transfer programs. Happy networking!

Fig. 2.2

3

STEP 3:

CHECK IT OUT

> When a man tells me he's going to put all his cards on
> the table, I always look up his sleeve.
> —Lord Hore-Belisha, British secretary for war,
> 1937–40

In Silicon Valley, John Sculley was considered a visionary, a model among businesspeople. As chairman of Apple Computer he symbolized what was best about high tech. To give you an idea of his status, he was the one chosen to sit beside the first lady during President Clinton's first major address to Congress.

One Friday in mid-October 1993, Sculley resigned from Apple. This was hardly a surprise; for some months he'd been scaling down. But his announcement the following Monday that he was joining Spectrum Information Technologies, Inc., was a shocker. This ten-year-old company had never shown a profit and was being sued by its own shareholders! When the press asked why, Sculley brushed it off, saying, "Sounds like you know more about it than I do."

The marriage lasted just 3 1/2 months, at which time Sculley quit and sued Spectrum's president for fraud. Sculley had chosen Spectrum for its patents on wireless computer communication. He had checked out the validity of those patents thoroughly. But when it came to lawsuits by Spectrum's investors, accounting problems, and an ongoing investigation by the Securities and Exchange Commission, apparently Sculley was far less vigilant.

This was national news. In the *New York Times*, Sculley claimed he was "blindsided." The business press wondered how a businessperson's businessperson could ignore the red flags and make such a deal. Actually, it was a classic mistake. He'd gotten too excited: He hadn't checked things out. Perhaps he thought because he knew part of the picture, the rest didn't matter, or didn't exist. From this we can all learn, for if it could happen to someone like Sculley, it could certainly happen to you.

"DO" DILIGENCE

Trust is *the* issue in every deal. Yet, like the proverbial elephant in the parlor, we avoid discussing it. We don't want to seem suspicious. We buy into glib patter and polished sincerity. Or we get greedy, careless, or just plain lazy. No matter what your excuse, remember: The most brilliant deal, superbly negotiated by top-drawer professionals, resulting in a signed airtight contract is of questionable value if the other side is too crooked or inept to deliver what they promise.

Due diligence is about uncovering the hidden risks in a deal *before* you shake on it. That way you can make a truly informed decision about whether to reject a deal or go through with it (provided you can negotiate an acceptable way to shift, spread, or control each risk).

SCREENING DEVICES: HOW TO SIZE PEOPLE UP

You can observe a lot just by watching.

—Yogi Berra

For now, forget the detailed projections, slick presentations, architectural models, and spiffy prototypes. Let's start with the obvious—what you see and hear.

Ten Ways to Give Someone the "Once-Over"

1. *Meet them face-to-face.* For this there's no substitute. Meet them on their turf, check out their offices, their clothes, their vibe. Someone's professional image should be consistent with who and what they say they are. If not, can you think of a plausible explanation that doesn't undermine their credibility?

2. *Second-guess your first impressions.* Research indicates that most of us form a strong opinion about a new person within seven seconds. Unless your accuracy is uncanny, that opinion is probably a cloudy mixture of personal bias, social stereotype, and raw intuition.

One way to uncover and explore your own biases is to consider whether a person reminds you of anyone.

3. *Watch out for snake charmers.* The sparkling eye contact, the facile rapport, the seductive voice, the winning smile . . . some people really know how to work you. Psychologists have proven that good-looking people usually have it easier. Know your own soft spots.

4. *Consider a simple reliability test.* My handyman, Chas Eisner, has a quick way to weed out flaky contractors: When he first contacts them, he speaks for only a minute before asking them to call back at a set time. Then he waits. After all, if they can't do even that right, how dependable could they be?

5. *Be wary of people who try too hard.* When someone goes out of their way to project one image, it often means they're exactly the opposite. This is one of life's little ironies and a clichéd media hook: the lascivious religious leader; the pilfering public official; the philandering "family" man. So the next time someone starts bragging about how honest they are, watch out. Methinks the lady (or the gentleman) doth protest too much.

6. *Watch the early signs.* Most people try to put on their best face at the beginning of a relationship. So if they lie or let you down then, expect only the worst if you climb into bed with them.

7. *Ask for written material.* Clothes may not make the man or woman, but business cards, catalogs, and brochures tell you lots about an outfit and its personnel, especially if those materials are shoddy or happen to be "unavailable."

8. *Observe how people act at different times and places.* Thomas Edison took prospective hires out to eat to see if they put salt or pepper on their food before tasting it. If they did, he concluded that they tended to prejudge, which he considered a poor reflection on their creativity. How does the other side behave on the golf course? Around the opposite sex? Under unusual circumstances? Get them out and about to see if you pick up irrational anger, disabling insecurity, or other clues to business or personal problems.

9. *Watch how they treat others.* One of my clients insisted on closing a deal with a guy who systematically swindled every one of his partners. Eventually, my client had a problem. Surprise, surprise.

10. *Don't show off how sharp you are.* Letting on how well you can read people can only make your target defensive. After all, once the enemy knows you've cracked their code, they'll stop transmitting (unless they really want to mislead you).

Body Language

Depending on which expert you ask, 70 to 90 percent of communication is nonverbal. The face, eyes, smile, handshake, walk, tone of voice, posture, positioning within groups, and even dress can tell you more about what's really going on than can any words. In many ways, if you learn to read the body, you learn to read the mind.

Figure 3.1 lists many common gestures and what they mean. Because human beings are instinctively wired to transmit and understand body language, mastering nonverbal communication is not as complicated as you may think. Just start paying attention. If you don't believe me, the next time you watch TV, turn off the sound. You'll be amazed at how much you'll be able to pick up . . . without the words. Here are a few more tips:

• If you're not sure what a gesture means, empathize. Go with your feeling response to what you see. Or ask the person for clarification.
• If the words and the body language are inconsistent, trust the body language.
• Read gestures and other cues in clusters. Like written or spoken language, body language has a grammar; don't read too much into one cue by itself.
• To create rapport, subtly mirror the body language of the person you're talking to.

As revealing as body language can be, avoid jumping to conclusions. Certain cues mean different things in different cultures. Gestures may also have a simple physical explanation. That person with their arms folded tightly against their chest may not be mad at you, just cold. And deep-seated personality traits invariably come through: Nervous people broadcast nervous cues, no matter what.

Questions and Answers

Above all, deal making is an exchange of words, an extended volley of Q&A. In the early game, your well-chosen questions will help establish rapport, assess character, and trade data. In the middle game, they'll direct the flow of info, reveal hidden options, and bring a deal into focus. And in the end game, you'll use them to persuade, pin down, and close.

BODY LANGUAGE BASICS

POSITIVE BODY LANGUAGE

CANDOR
uncrossed legs or arms; unbuttoned jackets; open palms

APPROVAL, SUPPORT
touching, moving closer, mirroring the body language of the other person, moving hands to chest

FLIRTING
preening, grooming

PREPAREDNESS
hands on hips, leaning forward, hand rubbing

CONFIDENCE
leaning back with both hands supporting the head, making a steeple with the fingers, raising the chin, putting the feet up, elevating oneself

NEGATIVE BODY LANGUAGE

GUARDEDNESS
crossed arms and/or legs

JUDGMENT
chin stroking, head scratching, hand-to-cheek gestures, cocked head, pinching the bridge of the nose

SECRETIVENESS
sideways glances, turning the body away, covering the mouth

DOUBT
rubbing behind the ear, rubbing the eyes

TENSION, INSECURITY
clearing the throat, fidgeting, tugging at pants while sitting, covering the groin area with the hands (known as the "fig leaf"), wringing hands

BOREDOM
drumming on the table, foot tapping, holding the head in the hands, doodling, blank stare

IRRITATION
rubbing the hair or back of the neck, short breaths, "tsk" sounds, kicking the ground or an imaginary object, finger-pointing

Fig. 3.1

How to Ask

Pick and choose from the following pointers. They won't all work together:

• *Act like a simple country boy.* This is a great opening tactic. People are less defensive and more open with someone who's friendly, easy-going, and nonthreatening.

• *Go fishing.* Chat them up. Get people talking with open-ended queries that usually begin with what, why, when, how, where, or who (our six honest serving men from Step 1). Avoid closed-ended questions (which can only be answered yes or no).

• *Ask early.* People are a lot less forthcoming once they start negotiating in earnest. For example, early in the interviewing process one of my prospective employers (foolishly) revealed (at my prompting) how desperate they were for someone with my experience. When we talked numbers, I successfully bargained for a much higher salary.

• *Ask twice.* J. P. Morgan said, "A man always has two reasons for the things he does—a good one and the real one." So after you get the good ones, ask for the real ones with: "And why else . . . ?" Also ask to hear the same story a second time—notice if anything changes.

• *Don't offend.* If you've got a query that's touchy, lay some groundwork by explaining why you're asking. Be diplomatic. Offer the other side a way to answer without losing face.

Here are some tougher approaches:

• *Let them know up front you'll check everything.* This is a great way to discourage lying. Unless their statements are hard to verify or they're fools or master cons, they're well advised to be truthful.

• *Ask questions to which you already know the answers.* You may learn more from their wrong answers than their right ones. This sort of testing is a classic private-eye ploy.

• *Try the sneak attack.* If you need to confront, consider surprising the other side with a direct question. Listen to their verbal answer, but really scrutinize their *nonverbal* reaction.

• *Be wary of information given too easily.* Be suspicious of what you learn under odd circumstances, such as what's "mistakenly" left out for you to see. Planting bogus battle plans on the corpse of your dead lieutenant is a cheap but sometimes effective maneuver.

• *Make a deliberate mistake repeating back some information.* Private investigators use this to detect phony identification. If the other side doesn't catch the error, you know something's up.

How Not to Answer Questions

You can learn a lot about how to be evasive by watching any competent politician in a jam. When you're being questioned and need to duck tough queries, you might:

- answer another question
- answer incompletely
- overanswer by being way too comprehensive
- disregard the question
- answer with another question
- counterattack
- tell a joke
- tell a story unrelated to the question
- reword and reframe the question
- not answer

How to Listen

Finally, and most important, listen. President Franklin Roosevelt used to delight in greeting guests at White House receptions with a smile, a handshake, and the following: "How do you do? I've just murdered my grandmother." No one noticed, because no one was listening. The following rules are deceptively simple, but extremely difficult to follow.

- *Don't interrupt.* Let the other person talk. You might be surprised at what people will disclose if you just let them finish.
- *Concentrate.* Don't allow yourself to be distracted by externals, or by your own inner dialogue. Stay present.
- *Use the power of silence.* Most people feel so uncomfortable with long pauses that they'll strain to fill them. Talk less and your opponent may tell you more (about what you'd really like to know).
- *Listen actively.* When the person is finished, reflect back what was said. If you need it, ask for clarification. Take responsibility for understanding the message.
- *Listen with your gut.* Empathize. Listen for feeling content as well as literal meaning. Use your skill at reading body language and other nonverbal cues.
- *Don't let your biases get in the way.* Do your best to be objective.

After you leave the encounter, consider what you heard and what you felt. Want one more interesting question to ponder? Ask yourself: What did the person *not* talk about?

References

"I've never seen a bad résumé" is every personnel director's standard quip. Likewise, most executives steeply discount the personal reference. Who'd volunteer a recommendation that's less than sterling? Also, you never know whether the reference is trading a favor, has an ax to grind, or is ducking a lawsuit for being either too honest or not honest enough.

Still, call your references anyway. One congressional study estimates that more than 500,000 Americans are running around with phony (or at least highly dubious) academic or professional credentials. It's worth your time to corroborate basic facts. On a good day, you'll get some honest answers or telling hints. If the references are top-drawer, you'll know you're dealing with a real player. To make these chats as fruitful as possible:

- *Consider the source.* Of course someone's mom is going to say much nicer things than their warden. Probe the relationship between the person you're checking and the reference. If you're in touch with an organization, make sure you're talking to the person who knows them best.
- *Prepare.* The reference is doing everyone a favor. Respect their time by having your questions ready.
- *Use your professionals to talk to other professionals.* Communication often runs more smoothly between members of the same occupation. Besides, your lawyer, accountant, or other expert should know which questions are really important.
- *Dig.* Review the tips about questions, particularly about asking open-ended ones, and listening. Don't be shy about asking pointed questions. So what if So-and-so is great? Ask the reference if they'd do business with him or her again. At the end of your talk, go fishing with this query: "Anything else I ought to know?" You never know what you'll catch.

Above and beyond all this, if you really want some dirt, be resourceful. Track down the references that were not available on request. This is a favorite of investigative journalists. Find and talk to that previous owner, to that unidentified source of financing, to the person's colleagues, and, above all, to a person's enemies. There are few better ways to triangulate someone's credentials. By the way, this kind of word of mouth can be just as revealing about organizations as it can be about individuals.

INSPECTION

When you buy, use your eyes and mind, not your ears.
—Czechoslovakian proverb

Famed Lloyd's of London took a beating when it agreed to insure certain parcels of "prime U.S. real estate." Almost all of it was in the South Bronx! Former hog dresser Anthony De Angelis ran a $175 million swindle, collateralizing loans with millions of gallons of vegetable oil that didn't exist. (Through underground pipes he moved a little oil from tank to tank, always producing full ones for inspectors.) Had auditors for Z Best bothered to visit Arroyo Grande, California, they'd have never found the eight-story building described in the company's second-largest contract; the tallest structure in Arroyo Grande has just two stories!

Of course, looking over the goods won't protect you from complex paper fraud or sleight-of-hand. Still, when you're dealing with something tangible, at the very least, go look at it, go count it, or go get a sample. If the other side objects, be leery. If they don't, at least you've done some due diligence, however primitive.

COOKING THE BOOKS: FINANCIAL STATEMENTS

Accountants are the witch doctors of
the modern world.
—Harman J. Miles, in Miles *vs.* Clarke

If you're vetting financial viability, financial statements will be your focus. A *balance sheet* is a snapshot of a company's assets and liabilities as of a certain date. An *income* (or *profit-and-loss*) *statement* details the flows of revenues and expenses for a given period. The *statement of changes in financial positions* shows where a company obtained its resources and what it has done with them. Like X-rays, financials reveal the internal workings and health of a living, breathing entity. Like X-rays, they can be analyzed properly and expertly or misinterpreted, poorly prepared, or just plain doctored.

How to Read Financial Statements

According to accounting theory, financials are usually prepared for "the general-purpose user," someone with a reasonably good understanding of business who will review the data reasonably carefully. Most deal makers fit this bill, but as you'll quickly see, the average businessperson can easily be misled by a crafty accountant. Some of what you learn here will help you ferret out fraud, fluff, and flaws, but you'll probably need your own financial wiz to really understand what the other side's financial wiz has done.

Between the Lines

Ironically, when scrutinizing financials one of the best ways to start is to ignore the numbers. First, know why the statements were prepared. For example, were they drawn up to attract a buyer for the business, for a divorce, for tax purposes, or to secure a loan? In each case, you can be sure the figures were massaged accordingly. Then, study the words of the text and the package as a whole. Some of this will be familiar from Step 2. In any event:

• Insist on financials audited pursuant to generally accepted accounting principles (GAAP); see page 30. If the statements weren't audited, find out why.
• Look for multiple balance sheets and profit-and-loss statements to see how the company has been doing over time.
• Hope for an unqualified opinion from an independent accounting firm of unimpeachable integrity (see fig. 3.2 and fig. 3.6).
• Check for a forthright letter free of obvious euphemisms from the company's president.
• Breathe easier if an independent audit committee was formed to prevent management from unduly influencing the auditors.
• Pray that negative information hasn't been disguised and buried in footnotes: for example, pending or imminent litigation, a sea change in accounting policy, explanations of unhealthy operations,

THE STANDARD OR CLEAN AUDITOR'S OPINION

The *scope and responsibility* paragraph:

"We have audited the accompanying balance sheets of _____ as of _____ , and the related statements of income, retained earnings, and cash flows for the years then ended. These financial statements are the responsibility of the Company's management. Our responsibility is to express an opinion on these financial statements based on our audits."

The *education* paragraph:

"We conducted our audit in accordance with generally accepted auditing standards. Those standards require that we plan and perform the audit to obtain reasonable assurance about whether the financial statements are free of material misstatement. An audit includes examining, on a test basis, evidence supporting the amounts and disclosures in the financial statements. An audit also includes assessing the accounting principles used and significant estimates made by management, as well as evaluating the overall financial statement presentation. We believe that our audit provides a reasonable basis for our opinion."

The *opinion* paragraph:

"In our opinion, the financial statements . . . present fairly, in all material respects, the financial position of the company as of _____ and the results of its operations and its cash flows for the year then ended in conformity with generally accepted accounting principles."

Any variation in this three-paragraph format is a red flag demanding further investigation!

Fig. 3.2

news of related party transactions, outrageous executive compensation packages, pro forma adjustments.

GAAP vs. *CRAP*

Accountants like to kid about the difference between GAAP (generally accepted accounting principles) and CRAP (cleverly rigged accounting principles). In practice, CPAs can and do use GAAP to dress up or conceal financial reality.

For starters, using GAAP to value assets can be highly misleading. You begin with what was paid for the asset (way back when), then depreciate it over time with standard formulas. The final number will be way off from the "truer" valuations that you may get from a professional appraisal, which may reference fair market value, replacement cost, or earning potential (see pages 10–13). Also, certain assets, such as favorable contracts or customer lists, and liabilities, like unfunded pension plans, may not appear at all. For instance, in its 1981 financials, the Johns-Manville corporation, then a leading producer of forest products and fiberglass, merely footnoted its soon-to-be highly publicized asbestos litigation. It set up no reserves to cover claims, and in 1982 the company went belly-up because of them.

GAAP gives CPAs options on how to report certain items. Depreciation varies depending on whether you use the *straight line, sum-of-the-digits,* or *double declining balance* method. Income and expenses may be recorded when actually paid or received, or when accrued. Profits on inventory sold may be figured under *FIFO* (first in, first out) or *LIFO* (last in, first out) methods. Certain costs may be treated as expenses or capitalized into assets. The *completed contract* or *percentage of completion* method may be used to account for contractual payments. Also, GAAP relies heavily on good-faith estimates—for instance, allowances for bad debts.

Each of these choices affects the bottom line, and the more aggressively a company exploits these options to manipulate its financial reports, the more cautious you should be. According to Irving and Loren B. Kellogg, authors of *Fraud, Window Dressing and Negligence in Financial Statements,* inventory is the asset account voted most likely to be manipulated, followed by accounts receivable, other assets, other intangibles, and prepaid expenses. Figure 3.3 lists some of the more common tricks of the trade.

WAYS TO COOK YOUR BOOKS

Timing Is Money
- deferring current expenses to another accounting period
- accelerating discretionary expenses to the current period
- keeping cash-received records open after the end of a period; closing disbursements records early
- depreciating or amortizing at different rates
- writing off future depreciation or amortization in the present accounting period
- liquidating reserves against anticipated returns to shift sales revenue to a later period
- recognizing revenue before it's fully earned or while significant contingencies exist
- delaying publication of financial results
- making unusual entries at or near the end of an accounting period

Through a Rose-Colored Visor, Darkly
- not writing off bad loans or worthless assets
- over- or undervaluing investments, intangibles, and other assets, especially difficult ones like excess inventory, private-placement securities, and contract rights
- ignoring liabilities such as long-term commitments, significant contingencies, or postretirement liability
- not making adequate provision for depreciation
- overestimating the collectibility of accounts receivable
- ignoring the obsolescence of fixed assets
- making bogus estimates, especially on interim financials

Let's See If It's in Stock: Inventory
- misstating inventory by counting empty boxes, altering documents, or adding in inventory that's not salable, for example
- valuing inventory at market price rather than cost

The Checks Are in the Mail: Accounts Receivable
- counting revenue based on goods shipped before a sale is final or based on merchandise shipped but not ordered
- considering sales on consignment complete sales
- ignoring buyers' rights to return merchandise

Fig. 3.3 *(continued on following page)*

Fig. 3.3 *(continued)*

- recording sales to buyers who are not likely to make payments because they don't have financing
- recording phony charges to customers

We'll Fix It in the Mix: Commingling
- mixing operating and nonoperating accounts
- folding a subsidiary's results into the parent company's financials
- paying debts out of the owner's pocket to inflate the price of a company before a sale
- retaining the main asset of the business in the owner's name
- borrowing through subsidiaries
- failing to separate unusual, nonrecurring gain or loss from recurring gain or loss; "restructuring" charges
- using equity or loans to fund dividend payments

Cosmetic Surgery: Hose Jobs
- using inflation to hide asset revaluation
- reporting quick gains from the sale of undervalued assets or from retiring debt
- burying losses under noncontinuing operations
- improperly capitalizing research and development, start-up costs, advertising, interest charges, repairs, and the like
- exchanging similar assets and counting what's received at fair market value
- keeping debt off the books

More Bad Stuff
- intentionally misapplying accounting methods to actual transactions
- taking aggressive positions on unsettled, difficult, or controversial accounting issues
- treating refunds as revenue
- entering phony or bogus transactions
- recording income on the exchange of similar assets
- failing to identify related-party transactions

Lack of Certified Statements

Many business opportunities involve smaller companies where certified statements are simply not available. Consider examining the outfit's books, ledgers, bills, invoices, bank statements, checks, and other supporting documentation thoroughly, with your own eyes. Of

SOME COMMON RATIOS USED TO ANALYZE FINANCIAL STATEMENTS

name	ratio	purpose
1. Return on Shareholder's Investment	net income to average shareholder equity	overall financial performance
2. Earnings per Share	earnings to number of shares outstanding	overall financial performance
3. Price Earnings Ratio	average market price to earnings per share	overall financial performance
4. Profit Margin	net income to net sales	profitability
5. Debt-to-Asset Ratio	total liabilities to total assets	solvency
6. Current Ratio	current assets to current liabilities	solvency
7. Acid-Test Ratio	quick assets to current liabilities	liquidity
8. Days' Receivable	accounts receivable to sales per day	asset turnover or efficiency
9. Inventory Turnover	inventory turnover to cost of goods sold	asset turnover or efficiency

Fig. 3.4

course, in these cases other forms of due diligence become even more important.

Crunching Numbers: Ratios

With business ratios, you can analyze and compare a company's performance over time against other companies in the same industry, or against other companies in general. Ratios will also alert you to upcoming problems, such as increasing inventories or a slowing in the collection of accounts receivable. Figure 3.4 lists some of the more popular ones. There are dozens of other ratios, many more specific and technical, and there's plenty of debate about which work best. Ratio studies are available from many different sources, such as Dun & Bradstreet, Robert Morris Associates, and branches of the federal government like the Federal Trade Commission and the Securities and Exchange Commission, as well as various trade associations, specialized accounting organizations, and universities.

Protection from Projections

While financial statements are historical, financial projections, sometimes called pro formas, forecast the future. Ordinarily they include a pro forma income statement, a balance sheet, and a cash-flow statement. The cash-flow statement is critical since it predicts the cash needs of the business at designated monthly, quarterly, or annual periods.

If ordinary financial statements require healthy skepticism, projections demand seasoned cynicism. It takes considerable technical skill to produce good ones, skill that is rarely demonstrated in practice. You've got to make precise assumptions and guesstimate hundreds of numbers, all the while minding the complex relationships among them. For example, a modest change in inventory may affect prices, labor, earnings, cash flow, taxes, or dividends. The better ones are integrated, with various statements and line items working together as a package; they also provide full explanations of the underlying assumptions on which they're based. As a general rule, never do a deal based on the other side's financial projections.

BEYOND THE BALANCE SHEET:
WARNING SIGNALS ABOUT A COMPANY

- a trail of bankers, lawyers, or other personnel who were fired or who resigned
- nepotism
- overreliance on a few customers
- management that is unaware of technological changes in the industry
- foolish diversification
- unfavorable union or other contracts
- unsalable or nonexisting inventory
- poor relocation planning
- no planning for executives' succession
- litigation history, pending claims, government investigations
- insiders selling stock
- extreme pressure to compete or survive
- part of a declining or saturated industry
- overly high profits or overly rapid expansion
- upcoming mergers or acquisitions
- weak internal controls
- lack of independent board members or audit committee
- unfavorable publicity
- restrictive loan agreements (e.g., working capital requirements)
- rejection by lenders
- lenders accelerating loan repayment
- delayed quarterly or annual reports
- too much public relations hype
- heavy intercompany transactions
- employment incentives of top management tied to stock prices
- large borrowing unrelated to its main area of business
- management forecasts that must be met
- unusual or complex transactions
- senior management that overpowers the directors, audit committee, and internal auditors
- financing not shown on the balance sheet
- principals with questionable backgrounds: megalomania; living beyond their means or other financial pressures; poor litigation history; drug, alcohol, gambling, or sexual addiction; criminal records

Fig. 3.5

BEYOND THE BALANCE SHEET: WARNING SIGNALS ABOUT AN AUDITOR

- long-standing relationship that may have made the auditor sloppy
- extreme career pressures
- the auditor or members of its firm have a financial interest or other business relationship with the company, one or more of its principals, or another company run by the same principals
- the auditor (or members of its firm) has a personal relationship with one or more of the company's principals
- the client is a significant source of business for the auditor
- the auditor's background is questionable: Watch out for those who are megalomaniacs; live beyond their means; are under extreme financial pressures; have a poor litigation history; are drug, alcohol, gambling, or sex addicts; or have criminal records
- no written statement from the accountant describing the scope of the engagement
- severe time or fee pressures to complete the assignment

Fig. 3.6

Beyond the Balance Sheet

If you're lucky, the figures, the ratios, the presentation, and your CPA will tip you off to any duplicity. But even if everything seems fine, look behind the numbers anyway.

Consider figure 3.5, which lists many of the factors that make companies prone to play with their books. Figure 3.6 is a similar list for accountants. You can't really evaluate financials without looking into the integrity and reliability of the principals of the business. This brings us to our next topic . . .

THE BACKGROUND CHECK

> It is not a fragrant world.
>
> —Raymond Chandler

Because it's usually done without the other side's knowledge, a background check is in many ways the most telling form of due diligence, a behind-the-scenes look at a person's or outfit's character and competence. Review the section on private investigators in Step 2 (pages 36–38). Although there's a lot you can do on your own, as with financial statements, professional help is usually the safer way to go.

Paper Trails: The Public Record

Jeffrey Rothfeder, author of the book *Privacy for Sale*, writes that there are over 5 billion public records detailing the personal lives of practically every man, woman, and child in this country. Figure 3.7 lists the basic ones. This is where a background check usually begins. The accessibility of these documents may vary by state and country, but by culling, cross-checking, and cultivating the bits of data that are legally available, the resourceful investigator can develop a picture of anyone's life. For instance, the header of a credit report may include a Social Security number, which reveals a person's former whereabouts or place of birth, where voting records may exist, which may produce past addresses, which can be run through reverse phone directories to list the numbers of former neighbors, who can be interviewed for additional information and leads, and so on. In one troubling experiment, *Macworld* magazine spent about $100 per person gathering public data on Clint Eastwood, William Hearst III (publisher of the *San Franciso Examiner*), George Lucas, Joe Montana, Janet Reno, Richard Rosenberg (CEO, Bank of America), and others. For each one they easily found almost all of the following: biography, birth date, civil litigation records, commercial loans, corporate relationships, driving record, home phone and address, marriage records, neighbor's phone numbers and addresses, real estate ownership, Social Security number, tax liens, vehicle ownership, and voter registration! Just because it's public and easy to get doesn't mean it isn't useful.

Do-It-Yourself Electronic Sleuthing

In the old days, researching public records was laborious, and therefore the province of seasoned detectives with plenty of time, hands-on experience, and a way with government filing clerks. Computers have changed all that. I'm sure *Macworld* magazine got most, if not all, of its information on-line. In any event, as the amount of data in cyberspace continues to mushroom, anyone with a modem can do lots of

BASIC PUBLIC RECORDS

Vital Statistics
birth certificates
death records
marriage licenses
divorce records
voter registrations
Social Security records
(postal) change-of-address forms
motor vehicles
immigration records

Assets
real estate deeds, transfers, mortgages
tax assessor records (for real property)
boat ownership
aircraft ownership
Uniform Commercial Code filings (records liens on physical property)

Court Records
criminal records
civil filings (e.g., bankruptcy, probate, tax courts)
liens and judgments

Membership and Related Records
military
professional licensing
academic records
other business licenses or permits

Public Directories
state and local government directories
phone books
crisscross directories (phone to address or address to phone)
professional or alumni directories

Databases
credit reports
biographical indices (e.g., *Who's Who*)

Newspaper or Magazine Articles or Announcements

Fig. 3.7

their own snooping and sniffing. Figure 3.8 lists some of the great (and better-known) places to start.

If you do go on-line, here are some tips:

• *Before you start, figure out what you want.* Sometimes you'd like everything you can find. Other times you should narrow your search to save time and money. Focus your efforts by picking the most unique search words possible.

• *Get as many identifiers as possible.* This is key to backgrounding individuals, especially those with common names. After all, you need to be sure you've got the right John Smith. The three best identifiers are full name, birth date, and Social Security number.

• *First ask how much it costs.* Searching databases can be expensive, especially if you're checking a large number of them. A couple of innocent keystrokes may cost you hundreds of dollars.

• *Know the limits of each database.* For example, Nexis probably won't catch a truly local story. Some databases (such as those of Dun & Bradstreet) tend to be self-reported, in that their information is based on what the companies themselves supply. So be skeptical of what you pull up.

• *Know what you're missing.* Checking a database can leave you with the false impression that you've really covered your bases. Make sure you've searched all appropriate time periods, sources, and geographic areas. Your subject may be clean in one state and have a glorious criminal past in another.

• *Try multiple spellings.* Databases are full of errors. If a search comes up dry, try spelling the name differently, reversing first and last names, or some other variations. Don't forget that names change.

• *Keep track of what you've already looked at.* There's no sense doing and paying for it twice. Also, your record of what doesn't come up is valuable in and of itself.

• *Find out if you're leaving a footprint.* Some databases keep track of who has requested what. You'll want to know in advance if that record will be available to your target.

• *Economize.* Are the rates cheaper at certain times? Is there a school or library where you can run searches for free? Is it more economical to start with one geographic area and then expand?

• *Learn the nuts and bolts of searching each database.* For example, find out how the software handles commas and periods, whether it is sensitive to upper- and lowercase letters, and whether it supports

---

THE INFORMATION SUPERHIGHWAY:
POINTS OF ENTRY FOR DEAL-MAKING DUE DILIGENCE

- CDB Infotek (800-427-3747) provides extensive on-line and user-friendly access to public records. Using CDB Infotek, almost anyone could search most of the items listed in figure 3.7.
- Dialog (800-334-2564) offers hundreds of on-line databases (including the full text of articles from newspapers and various periodicals) in dozens of areas, from law, news, and business to science and the humanities.
- Lexis and Nexis (800-227-4908) are also popular. Lexis is the on-line legal research tool of choice for attorneys. Nexis provides full-text retrieval from dozens of newspapers and magazines.
- DataTimes (405-751-6400) offers similar services to Dialog and Nexis.
- Check out the *Gale Directory of Databases* and *Gale's Information Industry Directory*, reference works that detail thousands of on-line, CD-ROM, and other electronic resources.

Fig. 3.8

any kind of wildcard searches. Many providers offer training. Take advantage.

- *Be clever.* You're playing detective, so think and make connections. Consider investigating people or companies that have relationships with your target. (More about this later when we background companies on pages 71–73.)

As wonderful as on-line access is, it's often just a starting point. For example, you may learn the who, what, where, and when of a lawsuit, but to get the whole story you may have to pull the actual case files at the courthouse or contact key players directly.

Backgrounding Identity:
How Do I Know It's Really You?

Do deals long enough and you'll run across at least a few card-carrying cons. Your business or social network will probably pre-screen them, or you'll brush them off instinctively, no harm done. As usual, basic backgrounding is a great preventative measure.

Social Security Numbers

Getting someone's Social Security number can be especially useful in weeding out a fraud. The first three digits indicate where someone was living when they got their card, the second two (the group number) can tell you when the card was issued. Tables exist that flag invalid numbers. So check the number and see if it's (a) real and (b) consistent with what you already know about the person. For instance, was it issued at an unusually old age? This is also a good question to consider as you're examining someone's driver's license. The number 078-05-1120 is popular, as it appeared on the sample cards contained in thousands of new wallets manufactured in the 1940s and '50s. Also, you should be aware that the system is far from perfect: Sometimes two people are issued the same number. So don't jump to conclusions.

Phony ID

If you're looking at other I.D. documents and a picture, physical description, or signature don't match, it's a dead giveaway. Check to see if the typewriter face on different parts of the card match, or if the name of the issuing agency is typed rather than printed. Examine the card for obvious physical flaws, such as photos that have been replaced or numbers or letters that have been whited out. Remember the old detective ploy: Read back some of the information with a deliberate mistake, and see if your suspect corrects you.

Creating a New Identity

The above techniques should screen out the amateur con. Detecting the professional imposter is much tougher. They often take the identity of someone long dead whose physical description matches their own. Creating a new identity usually starts with a search of birth and death certificates, preferably from another state. From there, obtaining a Social Security number, driver's license, and so on is easy. With do-it-yourself diploma kits, a prestigious mail drop, a Swiss bank account, and a few commonly purchased credentials (for instance, an offshore bank presidency or a coat of arms), the paper identity is complete. You'll need a pro (and the section entitled "Street Smarts" on pages 82–89) to protect yourself.

Backgrounding Money:
How Do I Know You're for Real?

Before a good salesperson pitches a product or service, they will "qualify" a buyer as being able to afford whatever it is that they're selling. Deal makers should take a cue from this. Find out early on if the other side really has the money to play. Otherwise, you may be wasting your time.

The Public Record
If someone's got assets, there should be evidence of it on the public record. In this regard, the owners of real estate, boats, planes, cars, or other items are almost always required to file specific documentation. Court records may document substantial judgments, tax liens, wage garnishments, and notices of pending lawsuits. Court files of your target's bankruptcy, divorce, or probate proceedings may be a gold mine of intimate financial detail. Filings with the Securities and Exchange Commission or analogous state agencies may contain financial data about the top officers, directors, and owners of publicly held companies. At times, the information available on government workers, officials, or general labor statistics may also come in handy.

If you can't find any trace of property yet believe the other side to be financially capable, they may have made a point of becoming judgment proof. This is a warning sign. Their assets may have been titled or arranged to shield them from legal attack. See pages 107–17. A large number of Uniform Commercial Code filings may also indicate trouble; these state and county filings put the world on notice that other creditors have first dibs on specific (i.e., other than real estate) collateral. Of course, real estate may be similarly affected. By the way, the type of property listed in a UCC can be revealing on a personal level: Is it a boat, a plane, a racehorse, a particular piece of artwork?

Credit Reports
Credit reports from the likes of TRW, Equifax, and TransUnion are the bane of consumer groups everywhere. Yet, although frequently inaccurate, they often do flag problem debtors. The Fair Credit Reporting Act (FCRA) loosely restricts their use to those with what is considered "legitimate" need, and although banks, department stores, landlords, and others rely on them heavily, not just anyone can order up someone else's report. In theory, you need to be a subscriber and hold writ-

ten authorization from the person you're checking. (But see "Spy vs. Spy" below.) Credit reports are also great for other background information, such as previous addresses, birth date, Social Security number, tax liens, and bankruptcies. However, they're not designed to cover everything: for example, pending litigation or related business entities. So keep snooping. By the way, credit inquiries leave a footprint. Your target can check to see who's been requesting his or her report, and so can you.

Personal Checks

With *merchant check verification* (or some similar service) a bank can, at the moment of your call, tell whether a particular check would clear. The problem is that by the time you get down there to cash it, it may not. A general banking reference or, of course, a cashier's or certified check is safer, although even then you could still be dealing with a counterfeit.

To spot phony checks, look for a difference between the amount written and the amount in figures, erasures, different typefaces, embossed or raised lettering, odd paper, or the absence of a transit number, which consists of nine digits preceded and followed by a stop symbol—an upright dash with two dots.

Backgrounding Character:
How Do I Know You're Not a Crook?

Although they're tricky to research thoroughly and may require a personal perusal at the courthouse, court records are a must-see if you want to check someone's basic honesty. For starters, you want to know if the other side has a criminal record. Records of convictions and pending prosecutions should be available, and although acquittals and charges that were dropped generally are not, there may be other ways to find them, such as through police or sheriff's departments, local newspapers, and special-clippings libraries.

Civil court filings are just as important as criminal ones. If the other side has been the plaintiff in a long list of lawsuits, you know they're litigious. If they're defending multiple lawsuits, find out why. Read the pleadings. Are their arguments principled? What other leads do the files provide? Bankruptcies are especially relevant. Also, see if you can find out about cases that were settled out of court. And if you want some real dirt, speak to the people on the other side of each lawsuit.

Spy vs. Spy

So far, pretty much everything I've shared here is legal. But there are also huge gray and black markets for information. As privacy expert R. E. Smith writes, "For very little cost, anybody can learn anything about anybody." Leaks at credit bureaus, credit card companies, utilities, banks, the IRS, and other government agencies mean that your tax returns, credit card purchases, loan applications, telephone records, bank balances, unlisted phone numbers, and post office boxes are all for sale. Private investigators rhapsodize over the juicy leads they find picking through a target's garbage. Reverse phone directories make it simple to talk to anyone's neighbors. Through pretexts, detectives craft carefully staged scenarios to chat up potential sources for information. And once you enter the world of electronic surveillance through, let's say, remote listening devices, hidden cameras, and "truth" phones with built-in lie detectors, privacy becomes a joke.

Today's fierce debates about computer privacy, mailing lists, telephone solicitation, caller ID, and access to medical, financial, and other personal data can only give the deal maker ethical pause for thought. When *you* need to know, you want the right to know everything. When you're the target, no privacy advocate can be too protective. If we had cheaper, speedier, and more reliable justice, we might not need to defend ourselves with comprehensive background investigations. But we don't. I'm not saying anything goes, and I certainly don't advocate using an illegal wiretap in your next big deal . . . but I sure would understand why you might wish you could.

Backgrounding a Company

In some ways, backgrounding a business is easier than backgrounding a person. There's simply more on the public record. In other ways it's harder; corporate and other business forms can conceal much, and it may take lots of patience, persistence, and analysis to peel away a legal facade. At the very least, this kind of backgrounding does let you confirm that people are doing business in the form they say they are: as a corporation or a limited partnership, for instance. See figure 3.9 for some ideas on where to begin.

To screen out fly-by-night entities, watch for companies that rely on mail drops, temporary suites, remote call forwarding (hard to find out

---

BACKGROUNDING COMPANIES: SOME PLACES TO START

- Filings with the secretary of state or Department of Corporations in each state should reveal the names and addresses of past and current owners, principals, attorneys, agents for service or process, and so on.
- Sales and marketing materials: brochures, annual reports, advertisements, listings in the Yellow Pages, trade show handouts
- Direct observation of company premises, including lobby or floor directories, packing materials, and instruction manuals may reveal former names or other leads or inconsistencies.
- Word of mouth from current or former officers, directors, managers, employees, attorneys, accountants, bankers, suppliers, customers, and (with a grain of salt) competitors
- Securities and Exchange Commission filings such as quarterly and annual reports, the prospectuses, and proxy statements are a wealth of information. Don't forget state securities filings, either. Have there been any violations?
- Business directories from Dun & Bradstreet, Standard & Poor's, Moody's, as well as the Thomas Register detail basic information about the day-to-day business of a company (e.g., sales figures, goals, size, affiliations).
- Newspaper and magazine articles, press releases
- Brokerage house reports
- Credit reports through Dun & Bradstreet or TRW; the restrictions that apply to accessing individual reports don't apply here.
- Consumer protection organizations, the Better Business Bureau
- Trade and licensing organizations
- The applicable federal, state, or local government agencies the company deals with; for example, on the federal level, HUD (Housing and Urban Development), GAO (General Accounting Office), DOD (Department of Defense), and EPA (Environmental Protection Agency). Has the company ever been punished or investigated for violations?
- The Basic Public Records that apply (see fig. 3.7), such as real estate deeds, court records (from pending litigation to outstanding judgments), boat or aircraft ownership, UCC filings, and reverse phone directories.

Fig. 3.9

from the phone company) and post office boxes. Remember that companies are made up of people. So draw connections between what you pull up on the individual and what you pull up on the entity. For instance, companies in the spouse's or kids' names may flag hidden assets.

LEGAL DUE DILIGENCE

If he would be a great lawyer, he must first
consent to become a great drudge.

—Daniel Webster

Generally, you save legal due diligence for last. All your investigations lead you to believe that your deal should work. So now you bring in the lawyer(s) to put everything under a microscope.

Figure 3.10 is just the outline of a legal due diligence checklist for a large corporate deal. It'll give you an idea of what an enormous task this can be: A comprehensive list would go on for pages. You should scrutinize not only the other side for all the legal headaches you might inherit, but the transaction itself to make sure it doesn't run afoul of corporate, securities, antitrust, environmental, or a myriad of other laws. Of course, not every item listed will be relevant to a given deal. In little deals, most won't apply at all. But as usual, it's always good to have a checklist.

Legal due diligence is highly technical. There is almost no place for the do-it-yourselfer. The bigger and more complicated your deal, the more legal specialists you'll need. But be warned: An overly cautious attorney can make a career out of the due diligence on a single deal. So, as the process unfolds, make your lawyer(s) explain the risks they've found as well as the risks of forgoing further investigations. Then, *you* make the call. Many times, you don't have to turn over every stone, pebble, and grain of sand. Also, coordinate your professionals to avoid duplicating work. Although the brunt of due diligence falls on the buyer, a seller had better pay attention if he or she doesn't want to be sued by someone who thought they were getting something they weren't.

Title and capacity or authority are two legal concerns common to almost every deal. Because a passing acquaintance with their intricacies is important for every deal maker, we'll take them in turn.

A "BRIEF" CHECKLIST FOR CORPORATE DUE DILIGENCE

A. Corporate Books and Records
   1. articles of incorporation
   2. bylaws
   3. minute books
   4. all current and prior addresses, fictitious business name statements
   5. stock ledger books
   6. agreements affecting transfer or voting rights
   7. options, warrants, calls, and the like
   8. federal and state securities filings
   9. annual reports and the like
B. Financial Statements
C. Federal and State Tax Returns
D. Other Applicable State and Governmental Filings
E. All Licenses, Permits, and Franchises
F. Litigation
   1. pending
   2. threatened
   3. administrative proceedings
   4. outstanding judgments
G. Real Estate
   1. ownership documents
   2. mortgages, liens
   3. leases
   4. environmental, hazardous materials
H. Personal Property
   1. equipment
   2. motor vehicles
   3. security interests
I. Intellectual Property
   1. copyrights
   2. trademarks
   3. patents
   4. trade secrets
J. Investments
K. Potential or Actual Bad Debts
L. Loan Documentation
M. Insurance Policies

Fig. 3.10 *(continued on following page)*

Fig. 3.10 *(continued)*

N. Key Contracts
    1. officers, directors, shareholders
    2. brokers
    3. government
    4. suppliers
    5. customers
O. Labor Law Compliance
    1. worker's and unemployment insurance
    2. OSHA
    3. fair labor standards
    4. employee benefit plans

Title: How Do I Know You Really Own That?

Obviously, before anything changes hands, one must be sure who it really belongs to in the first place.

Real Estate

The log cabin where Abe Lincoln was born is an American icon. But most people don't know that it was the subject of lawsuits over title which eventually drove the Lincoln family away.

Title simply means legal ownership: who has what rights in a piece of land and for how long. Actual physical possession tells you little. If you want to make sure you're getting what you're paying for, you need to have someone visit the local county recorder and study the chain of title for that parcel. This includes deeds, liens, mortgages, and other encumbrances on file.

In most cases, these public records do not lend themselves to user-friendly searches. They may not indicate easements, claims by adverse possession, mechanics' liens, boundary disputes, or zoning problems, among other things. Also, a basic search offers little protection against forged or last-minute filings, grants that aren't legally valid (for example, the grantor was a minor or an incompetent), clerical errors, or lost documents. To top it all off, local law may force you to search back as far as fifty years before it will deem a title to be clear. Because clearing a chain of title can be so treacherous, it is a job generally handled by specialized title companies.

Even title insurance, the most common solution to these and other problems, has its limits. Basically, it protects you and/or your lender from claims that the seller didn't own the property they just sold you. It won't make defects go away; it simply provides (limited) financial coverage if a claim comes in. Like other insurance policies, title insurance is riddled with technical conditions, exclusions, and exceptions. (See pages 93–100.) Fortunately, many of these are routinely eliminated if your lawyer or other representative knows what to ask for, which they should. Also, for many reasons, you may not get hit with a claim for years. So find an insurer that is likely to be rock solid for a long time to come.

Intellectual Property

In our technology-driven world, copyrights, patents, trademarks, and trade secrets may be a company's most valuable assets. Like real property, ownership of intellectual property (except trade secrets and the like) is on record; the Library of Congress holds records of copyrights and the U.S. Patent and Trademark Office holds records of patents and trademarks. As with real estate, title searches are tricky. There are some other special twists here.

Naively, many companies have not recognized how precious intellectual property rights are, much less done anything to legally protect them. This can lead not only to misunderstandings between buyer and seller as to who owns which rights but to nasty third-party lawsuits as well. Also, each form of legal protection has its limitations. For example, copyright does not protect ideas, only their expression; trademark rights in the U.S. may flow to those that use a particular mark even before there has been a public filing; trade secrets are vulnerable to reverse engineering; and filing for a patent entails public disclosure of technical secrets. Finally, as a practical matter, you really can't assess the value of particular intellectual property rights without examining the marketplace as a whole. For example, are developing trends about to make an exclusive technology obsolete? Is a competitor aggressively taking out patents to corner a market? Are separate licenses for several distinct intellectual property rights necessary for a particular project? Factor in the intellectual property laws of other countries, filing deadlines, and piracy, among other things, and the analysis becomes complicated indeed. As you might gather, you'll need experts to protect you.

Other Stuff

To a greater or lesser degree, the legal ownership of certain kinds of physical property can also be verified. Motor vehicles may be registered with the state, aircraft with the FAA. For horses, registries like the Jockey Club, the American Quarterhorse Association, and the Arabian Horse Registry of America can give good, but not always conclusive, evidence of title.

In any event, find out if there's a public record, registry, or other organization that keeps track of the good or property you are dealing in. For big-ticket items, check UCC filings to discover if any creditors have superior rights. Even a simple document, like a bill of sale, can be a good starting point. If you uncover other wrinkles, like that the original came from a bankrupt trying to outwit creditors, a spiteful spouse, a thief, a minor, or an incompetent, avoid the deal or get some legal advice to see if you can work around the problem. (See below.) Many classic swindles are based on selling something the con only *appears* to own. By now, you should know better.

Capacity and Authority: Do You Have the Right to Make This Deal?

Just because a person is physically capable of signing on the dotted line doesn't mean they have the legal right to bind themselves or others. The onus is on you to find out. Here are some typical problems:

Corporations and Other Business Entities

"President," "Vice President," "Chief Financial Officer": Titles for corporate officers are impressive, but they don't always grant the authority they imply. To really know who holds the power, you must check that particular state's corporate laws and that particular corporation's articles of incorporation, bylaws, and minute book. Otherwise, a corporation looking to renege on a deal has a potential easy out: The officer who agreed to it exceeded his or her authority. One way to protect against this is to require copies of a board of directors' resolution authorizing the deal, before that deal closes. Among other things, that resolution should be certified by the corporation's secretary and recite that the board meeting was correctly noticed with a quorum present.

Dealing with individuals who claim they represent partnerships, limited partnerships, trusts, or even other individuals (such as agents or guardians would) raises similar questions. As with corporations, examine the legal instruments that support such assertions or get written corroboration from their principals. If things don't go your way, the law will usually back you in relying on someone's *apparent* or *implied* authority (both legal terms of art) in a good-faith transaction in the ordinary course of business. But you may find yourself in court arguing complicated questions of fact and law. For example, did that particular organization hold the person out as having authority? Were higher-ups aware of what was going on? Do these people or companies normally do business that way? Should you have known better?

Powers of Attorney

These days, powers of attorney come in many flavors, including financial, health care, durable, general, limited, and springing. Each state has its own law on the subject, and sometimes knowing whether to accept one can be a real problem. For example, what if the person who granted the power of attorney was incompetent? What if the document itself is a forgery? What if the wording is ambiguous? Even if you know the person who granted it, how can you be sure it hasn't been revoked?

There are a few things you can do to cover yourself. Verify it with the person who granted it. Read the wording carefully to make sure it gives the power the attorney-in-fact claims. Check to see if it's been signed, dated, notarized, witnessed, and/or recorded; some state laws require one or more of these. In many states you won't be liable if you act on a power of attorney before you've been notified that it's been revoked; but look for language in the document to that effect anyway. If all else fails, just refuse to honor it; but make sure you're not violating any state laws that don't allow this when the power of attorney is in official form.

Of course, the preceding discussion is all about the other side's power of attorney. If you're granting one, be very careful about when, for what, for how long, and to whom you give it.

Spouses

Common sense tells us that determining who has the last word between husband and wife is sticky, both psychologically and legally. Obviously, if you're buying an asset that's in both names, get both to sign off. But even when that's not the case, and especially if the parties are separating or divorcing, play it safe. Get both spouses to say yes in writing anyway.

Bankrupts, and Those on the Way

If the other side is making a deal to stymie their creditor(s), they can end up getting you in trouble also. See the section on fraudulent conveyances on pages 108–109, especially the discussion about "badges of fraud."

Minors, Incompetents, and Drunks

According to *common law* (the law of England and the American Colonies before the Revolution), children, lunatics, and drunks were not considered to have the mental capacity to make a deal. Basically, these laws still stand today.

Generally, minors, drunken people, and incompetents who haven't yet been declared so by a court can, at their option, renege on a contract; in fact, some courts have held that a deal with an adjudicated incompetent with an appointed guardian is void from the get-go. If you make a deal with someone who's soused and they promise to honor it (or don't renege on it) after they sober up, then they're *on* the hook. By the way, a right to void a deal doesn't mean that these classes can simply wash their hands of a deal at will. Many times, they'll still have to reimburse the other side.

As usual, knowing who you're dealing with is your best defense. Here are some other ideas: With minors, having them represent they're of age will give you a better argument that they've defrauded you, should you end up in court. In some states, getting the parent to sign off on the contract, or on some form of guaranty, will also help. A few states, notably California, provide for court approval of certain minors' contracts in the entertainment industry.

With incompetents, keep the contract wording simple. Leave blanks to fill in so they can demonstrate their lucidity. Their being represented by a lawyer will also help. If some kind of guardian is involved, get your lawyer's opinion as to the scope and validity of the guardian's authority. In any event, if you end up litigating competency, the deal's fairness will be a key issue. In other words, if the judge or jury concludes that a person would've had to have been crazy to make that deal, then they probably were!

4

STEP 4:

MINIMIZE RISK

Progress always involves risks. You can't steal second base while keeping your foot on first.

—Frederick Wilcox

The perils of everyday life—disease, accidents, acts of God, crime, and the like—circle us constantly. Whether the loss is tragic or trivial, in our universe risk, ironically, is a "sure thing." So we shrug, sigh, and do our best. We prevent what losses we can, and we pay through the nose for life, health, automobile, property, disability, and other insurance policies. That much is simple.

Is risk in deal making more complex? You bet. Multiply the infinite unpredictable and potentially devastating probabilities of nature, the marketplace, and current events against the omnipresent risk of deception, the risk of your or the other side's incompetence or inability to perform, the risk of being sued, the risk of your own poor judgment, the risk of missing a better opportunity, the risk of moving too quickly, and the risk of hesitating, to name a few, and you begin to appreciate just how much can go wrong!

What You Already Know About Managing Risk

In every deal there are many ways to minimize risk. Actually, if you've applied Steps 1, 2, and 3 you've already done a lot to diminish your downside. Let's recap:

1. Step Back from Risk
By determining your goals, you've eliminated the risk of making a deal that can't give you what you really want. By analyzing value, you've

lowered the risk of making a deal that isn't worth it. By engaging your creativity, you've reduced the risk of missing better alternatives.

2. *Get Help* with Risk

Professionals make the big (and medium) bucks protecting you from the vicissitudes of the big bad business world. Although no expert can think of everything, their experience and skill at minimizing your risks are crucial to their bottom line and to their malpractice coverage.

3. *Check Out* Risk

In many ways, checking things out thoroughly before the fact is the very best insurance policy you can buy.

■   ■   ■

Now in Step 4 we learn specific techniques to manage the common risks that confront every deal maker. Basically, it all comes down to this: Either you check risk by controlling the outcome or you redistribute it by shifting, spreading, or insuring it. By the way, this is a particularly good place to apply the creativity exercises we learned in Step 1. Keep this in mind if you have trouble finding a practical solution.

STREET SMARTS 101: HOW TO CONTROL YOUR DEAL

> Common sense is not so common.
>
> —Voltaire

Let's talk down 'n' dirty deal-making self-defense. You may think that some of what follows is trite, but I assure you, it's not. At times even the brightest deal makers lose their horse sense.

"Possession Is Nine-tenths of the Law": The Deal as Hostage Exchange

The law, we all know, is slow, expensive, and often unjust. Forget right and wrong; the one who's got physical possession, unless they're the defendant in a criminal trial, usually has the strategic advantage. For stripped of social niceties, business is war, and every deal is just a hostage exchange. And it's in that moment between the giving and the getting when you're most vulnerable.

Depending on which side you're on, time your deals so you get (or hold onto) as many marbles as soon as (or for as long as) you can. This is one of the most powerful ways to control the other side and make sure you get what's coming to you. For example, let's take money:

Money sooner is better than money later. Once you have the dough, you've completely eliminated the risk of not getting paid. It's that simple. Also, deposits, advances, and front-loaded payment schedules test whether the other side is real. So unless you're staggering your income for tax purposes, get as much of your money as soon as you can.

Get your money at the source. Paul could wait for John to get his money from Peter, but if I were Paul I'd rather deal directly with Peter. The names may be confusing, but the lesson is easy. Go upstream whenever you can.

Get the best money you can. There's money . . . and there's MONEY! Cash is safer than a check, a certified check is safer than a basic personal one, and anything is better than a verbal IOU.

Don't spend money you don't have. If your project involves financing from a third party, don't make outside commitments until you've got the green in hand. Otherwise, you may be left twisting in the wind. Here's a corollary:

Don't throw good money after bad. If you're the moneyman, you've got to monitor your disbursements and reserve the right to pull the plug should your trusted charge fumble the ball. Ask any construction lender or parent putting their kid through college.

Most deals are more than simple swaps, so you may need something a little fancier. Consider these two techniques:

Offset

Savvy purchasers know not to pay everything at closing because if a problem comes up later, they'll have little leverage against the seller. Instead, they insist on a right of *offset*, or the right to reduce the money owed by the amount of any problem liability. The impound accounts for taxes, insurance, assessments, and the like, which are common in real estate deals, all derive from this.

Escrow

Escrow is like having someone referee your swap. It's native to real estate but works well with any kind of property. Basically, along with formal escrow instructions, a buyer deposits money, and a seller a deed, with the escrow agent. Then, in accordance with those instructions, the escrow agent administers the dozens of maddening details (including filings, title insurance, inspections, financing, apportioning of taxes, rents, and deposits) that lead to closing. When everything's in order, the buyer takes title (the deed), and the seller gets the money. If you go this route here are a few suggestions: Choose a truly independent agent, one who won't favor one side. Escrow is all about putting a third party in charge of your exchange, so be psychologically ready to give up control of what you place in escrow. Prepare escrow instructions precisely. If the escrow agent is unclear about what to do, they may prefer to do nothing rather than risk a lawsuit from one side or the other. Also, know that if the deal comes unglued, a legal action called an *interpleader* may be filed, paralyzing the escrow agent until a court can sort things out.

One Day at a Time: Step Deals

Better to invest time, money, and effort in stages than to jump in with both feet and get burned. This is the idea behind the step deal. For example, a venture-capital firm will provide funds in several stages, from seed capital to prove a concept viable, to bridge financing just before a public offering. At each prenegotiated juncture it reserves the right to reevaluate and either cut loose or proceed.

Plan Your Escape (Clause)

When deals disappoint, having the built-in right to get out can be a lifesaver. This is especially true if your deal has any kind of time line, as most do. It can be a firm outside date after which all bets are off. Or you can set a performance standard or condition, for instance, "If gross sales do not equal at least X dollars within eighteen months, we have the right to stop funding." But see the note on terminating a contract on pages 104–105.

The Option

An option gives you the right to buy or sell something for a set price at some later date. For example, for $10,000 today (the *option price*), you give me the right, or the option, to buy your house anytime within the next six months for $200,000 (the *purchase price*).

Like the performance standard, the option lets you hedge your bets by leaving you an out. You don't have to exercise the option. It also: (1) protects you from escalating bids by locking in a price, and (2) *if it's exclusive,* lets you control something for a while for less than it would cost to buy it. Thus, Hollywood producers option the right to make a book into a movie, team owners option their players for additional seasons, and homeowners-to-be lease a house with an option to buy. The option is one of the most commonly used devices in all of deal making. They are even packaged and traded like stocks and bonds, that's how familiar they are to us.

Although there are only a few details to nailing down an option, I'm amazed at how often they're overlooked by the average businessperson. Study the simple table in figure 4.1, which outlines the basic points and the best-case scenarios for each side.

Figure 4.1 will help you better understand this device, but if you're

DEAL POINTS FOR NEGOTIATING AN OPTION		
	If You're Getting an Option	If You're Granting an Option
Who gets to exercise it?	only you can	mutual
Is it exclusive?	yes, to you	nonexclusive
Option period?	longer	shorter
Extend option period?	yes, several times	no
Option price	lower is better	higher is better
Purchase price	lower is better	higher is better
How much of the option price applies against purchase price?	all	none

Fig. 4.1

a novice, don't base your next option negotiation on it alone. For one thing, each industry has its own special way of resolving the issues outlined in the figure. Also, it's difficult for a beginner to imagine how these scenarios may play out in the real world. For example, a non-exclusive option is often of limited value since it doesn't prevent others from bidding or buying. Likewise, an option that must be exercised mutually may leave one or both parties with very little control. In negotiating price, there's often a trade-off between the option price and the purchase price; less money up front usually means a heftier purchase price down the road, and vice versa.

A right to extend a deal for additional time on the same terms is a close relative to the option. Think ahead. If you know you're going to need more time, ask for it up front. The legendary Sam Walton, the founder of Wal-Mart, wrote that his biggest mistake in business was not asking for the right to extend the underlying lease on his first store. Despite his success, when the lease was up, he had to move and start all over again.

Agreements to Agree

Even when they're not sure of the details, most deal makers try hard to lock in future opportunities and extend promising relationships. Here are four alternatives:

An agreement to negotiate in good faith in the future is just a fancy way of saying that everyone wants to do business but will hash out the particulars later. It's more a statement of goodwill than a binding agreement with strong legal teeth.

A right of first negotiation is just that. For a set time, it gives one side the exclusive right to be the first to talk turkey with the other. Although at times it may seem like a token concession or an inconvenience, in certain situations (and depending on which side you're on), it may be key. For example, by insisting on a right of first negotiation from the get-go, Edgar Bronfman, Jr. prevented a bidding war when he acquired MCA in 1995. Business analysts praised his negotiating acumen.

A right of first refusal obligates one side to offer the other the first chance to buy something at a specific price. If the other side passes, the first side can sell it to someone else, but not for less than their original offer.

A right of last refusal (sometimes called a *matching right*) gives the side holding it the right to match the last best bona fide outside offer on the table. By giving one side the last word, the matching right offers more protection than a first refusal. However, the other side can first (for better or worse) discover the true market value of what they're selling. A right of first negotiation and/or first refusal can be, and often is, combined with a matching right. By the way, if you pass on a first or last refusal, don't get snookered: Insist on seeing the deal that was actually signed to make sure it wasn't better than the one you were offered.

Monitor Performance

There's no point cutting a spectacular deal if you're going to let the other side bleed away your hard-won gains through deceit or incompetence. To the extent you control the outcome, you control the risk. So stay in charge. Here are some tips:

1. *Communicate clearly.* Be specific about all of your expectations. Make them part of the written contract. Put all of your instructions to the other side in writing. Minimize miscommunication and you minimize misunderstandings and eliminate hundreds of risks.

2. *Build conditions into your deal.* The condition is the deal maker's Swiss Army knife. Ideally, everything you must do should have a condition attached; if it's not met you're off the hook. The other side should never have an excuse for not performing. For example, when banks loan money to companies, the banks insist on tons of carefully constructed conditions (working capital requirements, limits on capital investment, limits on the payment of cash dividends, and so on) that give them the right to decline or call a loan at the first sign of trouble. On the other hand, the borrower must make payments no matter what (of course). Here's a quick tip: If the other side is building too many conditions into your deal, eliminate or have them acknowledge as satisfied as many as possible from the start. We'll return to the topic of conditions in Step 5 on pages 132–33.

3. *Make them get your approval.* Make key items subject to your approval. In a sense, it's just another application of the condition. Approvals are often hotly negotiated; see figure 4.2 for some tips.

4. *Inspect.* Drop by the construction site, pop in at your tenant, or stop by your franchise. There's no better way to really see how things are going. The law doesn't always permit such spot checks, but when you can, make these rights part of your deal.

TIPS FOR NEGOTIATING APPROVALS

1. The strongest approval rights are:

Unilateral   Avoid mutual approvals; they lead to deadlock. If an approval must be mutual, make sure you have the right to break the tie.

Express   Approvals sought or given should be clear and specific.

Prior   To avoid the "fait accompli," approvals should be obtained in advance.

Written   Get written approvals to prevent misunderstandings.

Also, a party can insist that approvals be placed within its "sole and absolute discretion" to prevent being questioned about its ultimate decisions.

2. When you're subject to the other side's approval, get them to:

Preapprove   To eliminate surprises, have them approve as much as possible as early as possible—in writing.

Set standards   Sometimes you can avoid malicious or arbitrary fiats by tying approval to some objective standard, for instance: Anything at least as good as such-and-such is automatically approved.

Making something subject to the other side's good faith and/or reasonable approval is weaker protection since they can usually cook up some reason for disapproving. Still, it's better than nothing.

Accept time limits   This can be loose. State that approval can't be unreasonably withheld or delayed. Or it can be tight. State that approvals must be given within a certain number of days (and that the number of days may also be reduced for specific emergencies).

Also, try to get the other side to agree that if they miss a deadline, everything submitted is automatically approved.

3. If you can't get (or don't want to give) an approval right, at least take (or consider offering) a right of consultation. It's weak, but it's better than nothing.

Fig. 4.2

5. *Let them report to you.* Why not make yourself the boss? Give yourself the right to manage the day-to-day business, to cosign the checks, to receive reports, to supervise and direct.

Get Collateral

From the skyjacker taking hostages to the local bowling attendant holding your driver's license, deal makers love collateral. Call it a *lien*, *mortgage*, *trust deed*, *hypothecation*, *security interest*, or *collateral*, the concept is the same. Someone who owes you promises or lets you hold some other property that you get to keep if they don't honor their word.

Giving or getting collateral is technical stuff. The creation of an enforceable security interest generally requires a formal agreement and an additional step called *perfection*, which usually involves a governmental filing, a special notice, or possession. You'll need a lawyer, and probably one who is a bit of a specialist, to do it right. Here are some other issues you'll confront:

- You may have the right to foreclose, but if the time comes, will you want to?
    - Will the collateral be worth anything?
    - How difficult will it be to get?
    - What will you do with it once you get it?
    - What can you sell it for?
    - Will foreclosure be your exclusive legal remedy, or will you be allowed to pursue others?
- You may not be the only one with a security interest in that collateral. If others have first dibs (legally speaking, higher priority), you need to decide whether to get in line or to insist on cutting in front.
- It's easy to lull yourself into a false sense of security about security, especially when the rest of the deal sounds great. You must check out collateral as diligently as the rest of your deal. Otherwise, it'll be a double disaster if the other side breaches and you're left with phantom, worthless, or unseizable collateral.
- Document your security interest. When you're dealing with collateral, don't even think about skipping this step.

Keep Your Secrets

Unintended or unnecessary disclosure of sensitive information can only undermine your negotiating position and your business. We'll talk more about this on page 129 in Step 5: Negotiate. Keeping your lips sealed is one of your best street-smart strategies. The Spanish have a saying about this: "Secrecy is the soul of business."

Have a Fallback

Plan for Plan B. Mapping out an alternative won't prevent bad things from happening to good businesspeople, but it'll definitely reduce losses. So keep your options open.

SPREAD IT: GET MORE PEOPLE ON THE HOOK

> He that is surety for a stranger shall smart for it; and he that hateth suretyship is sure.
>
> —Proverbs 11:15

The more people you can look to if something goes awry, the better off you'll be.

Sign 'Em Up: Make Them a Party

Make other responsible parties sign on the dotted line, right alongside the party you're primarily dealing with. That's exactly what a bank is thinking when it makes Daddy cosign for Sonny Boy's first set of wheels. It's the best way to rope another, hopefully more responsible, party into your deal.

If you can, make sure everyone on the other side is *jointly and severally* liable. In a contract these magic words are the legal equivalent of "one for all and all for one." They allow you to recover everything you're owed from each individual without the incredible hassle of suing all the others. Otherwise, you may end up in a hall of mirrors watching everyone exploit legal technicalities to make sure you get nothing.

The Guaranty

According to a Yale University study, the word *guaranty* is one of the twelve most persuasive words in the English language. In business, it is a pledge to perform someone else's obligation if they can't or won't. Thus, if you doubt the other side's ability, find the oldest, richest, and most honorable person or entity you can to back them. Such was the inspiration for Iacocca's great brainchild, the U.S. government's guaranty of $1.2 billion of Chrysler's debt.

Unfortunately, guaranties may be better in theory than in practice. For one thing, there are many different types; see figure 4.3. Choosing the wrong kind can leave you high and dry. More important, judges are notoriously sympathetic to guarantors; in many cases the law provides technical defenses that let them off the hook (for example, that the underlying deal changed, unfairly increasing their risk; that the person whose obligation they guaranteed didn't get the benefit of their deal either; or that the guarantor didn't receive notice of some event when it should have). Ergo, if you want your guaranty to hold up, hiring a careful attorney to draft an airtight document that eliminates as many of these defenses as possible right up front is crucial.

The Letter of Credit

A *letter of credit* (L.C.) is like a cross between a guaranty and an escrow. Here's how it works: By formal letter (L.C.), a creditworthy applicant authorizes a financial institution, or issuer, to pay money to the other side of a deal, the beneficiary, if the conditions set out in the L.C. are met. The letter of credit is a favorite in international trade. For example, an exporter doesn't want to ship unless they're sure to get paid; an importer doesn't want to pay unless they've got the goods. So the importer-applicant takes out a *documentary letter of credit* with a solid bank, instructing it to pay the exporter-beneficiary upon presentation of certain documents (such as a shipper's letter of instruction, export license, or certificate of origin) which verify that the goods have been shipped. The exporter presents the L.C. and the necessary documents to the bank. The bank pays the exporter, then forwards those same documents to the importer so they can pick up the goods.

Like guaranties, there are many varieties of L.C.s. Which one you use depends on your deal and the conditions that are agreed to for

---

BASIC KINDS OF GUARANTIES

An *absolute* guaranty
   is unconditional.
A *conditional* guaranty
   has strings attached.

A *general* guaranty
   will work for anyone who'll accept it.
A *special* guaranty
   is only good for the specific parties that are named.

A *limited* guaranty
   applies to one transaction or part of a transaction.
A *continuing* guaranty
   operates over a series of deals.

A *personal* guaranty
   comes from an individual.
an *institutional* guaranty
   comes from (guess what?) an institution.

A guaranty of *collection*
   can't be called in until you first sue the original party.
A guaranty of *payment*
   is much stronger, letting you sue the guarantor directly.

Fig. 4.3

payment. A *standby letter of credit* is especially handy. It can be drawn on as needed, such as if the other side defaults on the underlying deal.

Note that an L.C. is really three deals in one: (1) between the beneficiary and the applicant (the true underlying deal); (2) between the applicant and issuer (to reimburse the issuer if it honors the L.C.); and (3) the actual L.C. Theoretically, the issuer couldn't care less about the underlying deal. Absent fraud, if the L.C.'s terms are met, it pays. Period. Therein lies its strength and reliability: The underlying deal is independent of the L.C. But in the real world, it's not so tidy. If an L.C. is drawn after a deal explodes, an applicant may well sue the issuer, claiming, probably unfairly, that it should have watched the underlying deal and/or that the terms of the L.C. weren't met. Conversely, if a bank is unsecured and feels that an applicant is financially shaky, it may seize on some technical failure to meet the *exact* terms of the L.C. to deny payment. This happens a lot in the export-import world; by some estimates more than 50 percent of the time in the U.S. Thus, if you do opt for the L.C., get a solid issuing bank, have the letter *confirmed* (backed up by another bank), get a specialist to do the paperwork, and keep the terms of your L.C. crystal clear.

Bonding: Suretyship

A *surety bond* is the Rolls-Royce of guaranties. Like a guarantor, a surety is bound to answer for another, the principal. But gone are the legal loopholes. A surety's liability is joint, direct, and primary, just as if they had signed the original deal all by themselves.

There are literally hundreds of different surety bonds. Many are part of deals made by the government. *Official bonds* insure the honesty of federal or public officials, *license* and *permit bonds* (such as a *liquor bond*) force a business owner to comply with applicable laws, and the infamous *bail bond* is one of many *judicial* and *fiduciary bonds* required during court actions.

In the free-wheelin' deal maker's world, we see *contract bonds* most often in construction, guaranteeing the completion of bridges, sewers, highways, buildings, and other structures. *Supply contract bonds* guarantee delivery of prefab materials. *Bid bonds* guarantee that the contractor who wins the job will do it at the price bid. A *performance bond* guarantees completion of the work when he inks the deal. A *payment bond* insures that all labor and materials will be paid, and a *maintenance bond* is exactly what it sounds like. Bonds have been written for auctioneers, blasting and explosive contractors, maids, dog walkers, college students, fish removers, auto clubs, collectors of bird's nests; they've been issued for motion-picture producers (to make sure their films will be finished on time), for perfume companies running contests (to make sure that the prizes will be awarded), and even for escort services (to make sure that all services are "faithfully" performed . . . whatever that means).

Unlike a guarantor, a surety's job is not to wait in the wings but to prevent loss in the first place. Unlike an insurer, the surety collects fees not to create a pool to cover loss but to lend its name to a deal. Put another way, a surety is a police officer. And since this cop may end up answering for the bad deeds of its principal, it's going to make sure everything goes right, the first time. To that end, it'll also keep the risk squarely on the principal. If the surety must step up to the plate, the principal will be legally obligated to answer to the surety later. By the way, there's one other nice thing about a surety bond: It can be much easier than foreclosing on, managing, or disposing of collateral.

INSURANCE

> *Insurance, n.* An ingenious modern game of chance in which the player is permitted to enjoy the comfortable conviction that he is beating the man who keeps the table.
>
> —Ambrose Bierce, *The Devil's Dictionary*

Always Consider Insuring It

While no insurer will cover the general risk of making a lousy deal, sometimes it seems like there's a policy available for every smaller component risk that makes up a particular deal. Consider figure 4.4. Policies have been written on Jimmy Durante's nose, Betty Grable's legs, stud horses (in case they're impotent), and NASA's lunar lander; for lottery-ticket printers (in case they print too many winning tickets), to cover a target corporation's expenses to fight off a hostile takeover, and to protect Cutty Sark in case someone actually found the Loch Ness monster and tried to collect the $1 million advertised reward! There's even reinsurance, which is insurance for insurance companies. So whenever you, or your risk manager, insurance agent, or broker, identify a risk, always ask whether it can and should be insured.

Which Side Gets the Policy

Like taxes, insurance is a silent party to every deal. Which side gets and pays for it, who's responsible for deductibles, and how proceeds will be split are all points to negotiate.

The Certificate of Insurance

If you're the one who is supposed to take out the policy, you'll be in the best position to make sure it's done right. If not, you're exposed to a

INSURANCE FOR DEAL MAKERS

Accounts receivable insurance reimburses you if your records are destroyed and you are no longer able to collect what you're owed.

All-risk insurance is a general class that, unless specifically excepted, will cover every risk except the insured's fraud. Contrast this with insurance policies for specific perils, fire, hail, riot, political upheaval, and so on.

Business-interruption insurance will pay your overhead and the money you would have made if you shut down because of a casualty. Also consider contingent business-interruption insurance in case a major customer or supplier shuts down and extra-expense insurance to cover the additional money needed to operate after a casualty.

Casualty insurance is a broad designation covering injuries to life, limb, and, to some extent, property. Accident insurance is one example.

Credit insurance protects you from bad debts.

Crime insurance is just that. It covers losses caused by criminal acts.

Directors and officers liability insurance is like malpractice insurance (see below), but for corporate executives.

Employer's liability insurance guards employers from claims by workers that don't fall under worker's compensation insurance.

Errors and omissions insurance protects you from your own mistakes and oversights. For example, in the communications and entertainment industries, it covers companies from claims for libel, defamation, invasion of privacy, copyright infringement, and the like.

Foreign exchange insurance helps you hedge your bets against fluctuating currency exchange rates.

Guaranty or fidelity insurance is another broad classification that, depending on the policy, will cover losses caused by the dishonesty of employees, agents, and others in a position of trust; embezzlement; certain nonpayments by your debtors; and/or breaches of contract.

Key man insurance makes the business the beneficiary if a vital officer or employee dies or is disabled.

Kidnapping and ransom insurance can really pay off if key players are the victim of terrorism or extortion while traveling abroad.

Fig. 4.4 *(continued on following page)*

Fig. 4.4 *(continued)*

Leasehold interest insurance protects that great deal you made on your lease. If that space becomes unhabitable and you must move somewhere more expensive, this insurance will cover you. Rental value insurance is the analogous insurance for landlords.

Malpractice insurance protects professionals from their own negligence.

Mortgage insurance will cover your payments if you can't.

Partnership insurance, conceptually, is like key man insurance but among partners. Often, it's life insurance taken out to help the surviving partner(s) buy out the interest of the deceased partner(s). Similarly, in a closely held corporation life insurance may be used to fund buyouts; the corporation or each shareholder buys a policy on the life of every other in the amount necessary to buy out their shares under their shareholder's agreement.

Product liability insurance covers manufacturers and suppliers from claims that their products caused injury.

Property insurance is another broad category and first cousin to casualty insurance. It's applicable to (you guessed it) all kinds of physical property, such as crops, ship hulls, motor vehicles, or machinery.

Profits and commission insurance is great for the salesperson whose commission is at stake when the company he or she is working for doesn't deliver.

Title insurance protects you from claims that the seller didn't really or completely own the property they just sold you. It can also apply to intellectual property, such as a book or a trademark. Distinguish between a *certificate of title* and *insurance of title*. The former is really just an opinion that title is O.K., and the company is only on the hook if the opinion was negligent. With insurance of title, the company must pay off if title is faulty.

Worker's compensation insurance helps employers cover payments to employees injured on the job.

---

new risk: the other side's screwing up and leaving you bare (or scantily clad). To protect yourself, insist either on examining the policy yourself or on receiving a *certificate of insurance* from the insurer. The certificate will confirm the material points of the coverage: type of insurance, policy limits, exclusions, deductibles, beneficiaries, and so on. Make sure the policy or certificate provides that you'll be given adequate notice if premiums haven't been paid, if the coverage is changed, or if the policy is about to be canceled.

Check Out Your Insurance Company

Obviously, there's no point paying premiums to a company that's unreliable or teetering on the brink of insolvency.

Rating the Raters

Start with the services that rate insurance companies. A. M. Best is the most popular, offering ratings on financial strength from A+ to C. Standard & Poor's also hands out grades based on the insurer's ability to pay, though ratings are made only at the insurer's request. Some think that Weiss is the toughest; there's also Duff & Phelps and Moody's. For extra protection, check out the insurer's reinsurer and consider requesting a *cut through* endorsement so you have direct access to that reinsurer. However, know that these services are fallible: The same insurer may be rated differently by different services. Evaluations are largely based on data supplied by the insurance companies. Grades are deceiving in that A does not necessarily mean top-drawer. In 1994 Best rated 78.2 percent of property casualty companies and 65 percent of life companies A- or better. Finally, from time to time a company is declared hearty and hale one day, only to be pronounced dead the next.

Other Indicators

If you've hired a risk manager, agent, or broker, expect them to know the word on the street. If not, check out public filings. Pay special attention to the *convention statements* that are required by state law— the insurance equivalent of the 10-K annual reports required by the SEC from publicly held corporations. Also, go on-line, call state insurance offices, get personal references, and interview some key people at the company, like the claims supervisors you may work with. Here are some other good things to find out: Do they contract out parts of their business? (This may indicate a lack of control or service problems.) Are financiers backing away? Have relationships with lawyers or accountants been severed abruptly? (There may have been a fight over disclosure in public filings.) Are their rates too good to be true? Have they been in business less than five years? Do they have a reputation for being difficult about payment? Do you hear lots of complaints?

How to Make Your Best Deal with an Insurer

A leader in the investment banking community described the insurance industry as "the last vestige of totally obscured power . . . invisible, vast power." You don't need a Ph.D. in economics to figure out why. First, insurance companies know the odds; you don't. They make buckets of money insuring what will never happen. Today, American consumers pay 12 percent of their annual income to an industry that employs over two million people and controls over $800 billion in assets. Second, buying insurance is very emotional. An insurance agent will work your insecurities like Kenny G. plays the soprano sax. Third, the insurance industry is the Heavenly Father of fine print, lord and liege of the legal loophole. Every year insurance companies produce over a billion documents, a stack of paper 6 ½ miles high! Here's some advice on self-defense:

1. *Give yourself time to shop.*
   - Prepare early for renewals; get policies (or at least detailed binders) well ahead of each effective date.
   - Ask for as much advance notice of cancellation and/or non-renewal under your existing policies as possible.
   - If you have multiple policies, consolidate effective dates. Staggering the effective dates is a trick of the trade and is one way agents make it difficult for you to switch companies.
   - Avoid choosing January 1 and July 1 as effective dates—insurers tend to be overloaded then.

2. *Lower your rates with package policies.* Taking out a number of policies with the same insurer offers two additional benefits. First, if you have a dispute with your company, you'll have more leverage if you're a larger account. Second, you may avoid disputes between two different insurers (and potential gaps in coverage) when it's unclear which policy applies.

3. *Consider hiring a risk-management consultant.* Get them involved early. Find out, up front, if parts of your deal are uninsurable or prohibitively expensive to cover. An *MBA*, an *ARM* (associate in risk management), or a *CPCU* (chartered property and casualty underwriter) is a good qualification. Also, know the difference between an insurance

broker, who can shop among many different companies for your best deal, and an insurance agent, who works with only one but should know and work with that one really well.

   4. *Be vigilant about the written word.*

- Keep great records, including a list of everything that's insured, copies of policies, loss reports, and any audit or ratings adjustment statements. This will help you prepare for negotiations and will keep your insurer honest.

- If the company gives you an interpretive opinion regarding a certain coverage, confirm it in writing. Read about the reliance letter on pages 167–68.

- Triple-check your correspondence. Read all policies and binders carefully. Make sure they're absolutely accurate regarding who and what is covered, for how much, for how long, and so on.

- Renew on time. Don't give your insurer an excuse to deny you coverage.

- Report claims promptly. Again, don't give your insurer any excuses to drop your coverage.

- Don't lie on your application. Even if it has nothing to do with the claim that actually comes in, an insurer might argue that it does, and that they never would have issued that policy. This is an easy way for the insurer to either avoid paying or settle you out cheaply.

   5. *Control your losses.* Frequent or needless claims make you a lousy risk and increase your premiums. Companies will often recognize and give you a break for your preventive efforts. Some even sponsor programs to show you how to cut losses.

   6. *Beware of gaps in your coverage.* In the words of David Yaters, "An insurance policy is like old underwear. The gaps in its coverage are only shown by accident."

- Again, go through your policies with a fine-tooth comb. Know the exclusions; see if you can modify them, delete them, or buy more coverage. If the policy limits are too low, consider additional coverage.

- Watch out for *claims made* policies, which are coverages that apply only to claims arising and made while the policy is in effect. To really protect yourself, you may need *nose* coverage, for any preexisting claims, and *tail* coverage, for claims that come in after your policy expires. In fact, you may have to extend tail coverage indefinitely, often at rates that escalate sharply.

- Coordinate your umbrella and underlying policies carefully. Make sure there's no dollar-limit gap between where the underlying policy ends and the umbrella kicks in. Make sure the umbrella is no more restrictive regarding claims covered than the underlying policies.

7. *Get the correct amount of coverage.*
   - Don't double-insure. Consider all your policies. Are there overlaps you're wasting money on?
   - How often will you be subject to a deductible: once per location, once per occurrence, or once per policy? For you, less equals more (coverage).
   - Consider the cost of replacement policies. On heavily depreciated property or older items that still function well, insurance that pays only actual or market value is practically worthless.

8. *Negotiate price.*
   - Prepare accurate specs. Insurers use standard classifications to calculate rates. Ask your insurer to explain which classifications have been applied and how.
   - Compare alternative quotes at different levels of coverage.
   - Lower your premiums with higher deductibles. Generally, you'll come out ahead if you bear or coinsure the first portion of the loss yourself.
   - Also, reduce your premiums with longer *elimination periods* at the beginning of the policy. During these periods you (and not your insurer) bear the risk.
   - If the policy is set up so that premiums are estimates, check to see what your insurance company has actually earned and whether you're entitled to any refunds or credits.
   - Shop rates, not premiums. Don't get sucked in by low initial premiums that will be raised after the insurer collects more data.
   - Will your insurer let you defer premiums?
   - Look at the whole picture when evaluating price: tax consequences, the time value of your premium payments, cash flow, lost opportunities on investments—not to mention nonmonetary factors, like service.
   - Check the math.

THE AIRTIGHT CONTRACT

> The way to negotiate a contract is to pretend that
> you and that nice man across the table . . . are both
> going to die tomorrow, and your heirs hate each
> other's guts.
>
> —Frederik Pohl

Written contracts protect one party against another's faulty or convenient memory, and as a last resort, provide the footing necessary to
sue and win. In Step 6 we'll learn all about the process of documenting a deal. Here, however, we'll focus on the boilerplate, those endless
paragraphs of indecipherable legalese that are included in formal contracts to protect one side or the other against a host of specific risks.
Before we start, here are two warnings:

First, if getting a formal agreement is the only way you're coping
with the downside, your only upside may be a winning lawsuit—a
costly, time-consuming, aggravating ordeal that may leave you with a
Pyrrhic victory by way of a worthless judgment. Because few contracts are 100 percent waterproof, a clever attorney can usually poke
holes even in the best ones. As a practical matter, boilerplate is rarely
even mentioned until the main points of a deal are in place; even then
the principals usually ignore it, leaving it to their lawyers to hash out.
Thus, think of your long-form, formal contract as a great secondary
line of defense.

Second, what follows is just the fifty-cent tour through the what
and why of most common boilerplate provisions. Though it'll help you
better understand contracts and what they can do, it's not a do-it-
yourself blueprint. The effectiveness of these clauses depends on precise wording. Whether you're sending out the contracts or analyzing
those you receive, call your lawyer for help.

Party Hopping: Assignment

When your attorney pontificates about how "the law favors the assign-
ability of contracts," he or she just means that deals can be bought or
sold. Thus, for better or worse, you may end up in bed with a complete stranger. Like all things legal, the general rule is subject to
embellishment, elaboration, and exceptions galore. For example, the

term *assignment* really means two things: the sale to a third party of one side's right to receive something from the other, and/or the delegation to a third party of one side's duty to do something for the other. The law is much stricter on the latter than the former.

In any case, if you don't want your deal sold, say so in your contract: "Any assignment of this agreement by [the other side] is void." On the flip side, if you want the unrestricted right to sell the deal, you can spell that out too. You can even compromise: Just list which assignments and/or delegations are O.K. and under what conditions (for example, approval or notice).

Key Man Clause

If the only reason you sign with a big company is because of your relationship with a few individuals, what will you do if they split? Your protection is a *key man* clause, which allows you to walk away if those people quit or are fired. Companies don't like it, so it's tough to get. But try anyway. You'll score big points with your "key" people. *Change of control* provisions involving partnerships or corporations are similar, triggering buyout, termination, or dissolution rights if the original person(s) you dealt with no longer control the entity.

Make It Complete: The Integration Clause

Often the last provision in a formal contract, an *integration* or *merger* clause protects you from a claim that there are other parts to your deal that you didn't write down, or that somewhere down the line you verbally agreed to change things. In simple form it may read: "This agreement contains our entire understanding and cannot be changed orally." Before you include it, remember that it cuts both ways. If you think you'll be the one needing to claim that there's more to your deal than what's on paper, consider leaving it out.

Audit Clauses

If you're entitled to ongoing profit or royalty payments, an audit clause will give you the right to check their accuracy. Without it, you may have to sue to see the other side's books and records. If you're the one auditing, get frequent accountings, as well as the right to see whatever specific records you'll need to verify that you've been paid correctly. Also, try to get the other side to pay for the audit in the event that you turn up more than a 5 percent error. On the other hand, if you're the one to be audited, make sure you're given adequate notice, that the audits remain confidential, that the audits not be too frequent or too long or require you in turn to audit any third party on whom you relied in issuing statements or payments.

"Trust Me, Baby": Representations and Warranties

Puffing and exaggeration will always be part of deal making; but if prevarication's the disease, *representations and warranties* are the cure. We make the other side reduce to black and white that which it promises to be true, the facts we count on when we shake on it—for example, that the board of directors approved the deal, that the song really is original, that the premises will be up to snuff when we move in. These types of warranties are a close cousin to the consumer warranties for parts and labor that we all know and love. Only here the stakes are higher. Make a phony representation or warranty and you may get nailed for fraud, not to mention any loss related to your misrepresentation.

Reps and warranties (R&Ws) must be tailored to each deal. Complex deals mean comprehensive R&Ws and extensive negotiations. For example, a big corporate deal will include R&Ws on everything under the sun: accuracy of financial statements, payment of taxes, title to assets, insurance policies, customer lists, compliance with various laws, proper corporate formation and operation, stock and good standing of each party, zoning, inventory, patents, accounts receivable, lawsuits, trademarks, and so on. See figure 4.5 for another example.

Even though R&Ws flag problems and promote honesty, don't look the other way just because the other side swears it's so. In the real world, their dishonesty or negligence will become your problem . . . and your lead-pipe cinch of a lawsuit may be cold comfort. Even the tightest R&Ws don't replace due diligence, insurance, or any other risk-management strategy.

Get Yourself off the Hook: Exculpatory Clauses

Boilerplate is great for naked risk shifting. If the other side has got leverage, expect it to sell you the goods "as is," let you enter the premises "at your own risk," and boldly saturate its contracts with *dis-*

STANDARD REPRESENTATIONS AND WARRANTIES WHEN A STUDIO BUYS THE MOTION-PICTURE RIGHTS TO A BOOK

- that the author is the only author
- that the book is completely original
- that the author owns all the motion-picture rights in the book
- that the author has never before granted the motion-picture rights to anyone else
- that there are no outstanding or anticipated lawsuits regarding the book
- that the book is completely protected under U.S. copyright law
- that the title of the book may legally be used as the title of the motion picture
- that the book does not defame or violate anybody's right of privacy or publicity, copyright, or any other legal right
- that the studio's producing and distributing a movie based on the book will not violate any other person's legal rights
- that the author won't enter into any other agreement that may interfere with or devalue the studio's motion-picture rights in the book

---

Fig. 4.5

claimers, express *denials of warranties*, and *limitations on liability* and even place the onus on you to buy insurance. It can border on the unethical, outrageous, and even illegal, but like it or not, a party can, in many cases, contract away its responsibility.

The most celebrated of exculpatory clauses is the *indemnity*, the perfect accompaniment to many of the above "risk shifters" or any representation and warranty. Among other things, it offers protection from third-party lawsuits. In other words, if you've agreed to indemnify me and I'm sued by someone else because of the deal I just cut with you, you will pay a lawyer to defend me, as well as any judgment should I lose (God forbid). Lawyers love to haggle over this. Who controls the lawsuit? What if you want to settle and I don't? What exactly does the indemnity apply to? Does it take effect when I get a nasty letter, when I get sued, when I lose, or when I have to pay? Blah, blah, blah, blah, blah . . . Courts look on *contribution* favorably; each party bears a proportionate share based on relative fault.

A *notice clause* lays out with (stupefying) specificity exactly how the parties will exchange formal communications, including where, when, and how to send them; when they're effective; who gets copies; which ones can be verbal; and so on. Although notice clauses are not intended to be exculpatory, they can be used that way. Send a notice without scrupulously following the letter of the contract and your opponent may scream "Foul!" and declare your notice improper and ineffective. Seem crazy? Maybe. But with a bit of luck, the other side may blow enough smoke to get themselves off the hook, especially if they can argue that your improper notice put them at some disadvantage.

When Murphy Comes Calling:
Staying out of Court

"Better to enter a tiger's mouth than a court of law" declares a famous Chinese proverb. Although we can't eliminate conflict from even the rosiest relationships, contracts can be constructed to help us avoid silly lawsuits.

Think of a *notice and cure* provision as a second chance. Before the other side can sue, it first must tell you what's wrong and give you a chance to fix it. Generally, it doesn't apply to something that could never be fixed in time, such as the building you had for sale that just burned down, or to one side's flat refusal to go through with the deal (technically, an *anticipatory repudiation*). Although notice and cure can prevent a reckless declaration of war, it may also be abused if repeatedly invoked to buy more time.

A *termination* provision is just another name for an escape clause (seen earlier on page 83); if one side doesn't perform or if the deal doesn't go through for some other reason, the other can cut loose. Its second cousin is the *suspension*, which gives one party the right to put the deal on hold while the other gets its act together. Suspension works well as the precursor to termination and as a way to cope with *force majeure*, which refers to acts of God, like tornadoes, earthquakes, and fires. On the other hand, anticipating all the consequences of a termination (like who gets to keep what, who has to pay what, what each side can do after the deal is over, and whether it all depends on whether it's based on one side's default or disability or on force majeure) is tricky. Sometimes industry custom will guide you; other times you'll have to be creative.

A *liquidated damages* clause fixes the amount of money one side must pay if it breaches. That way the parties don't have to argue about it at the time. If the clause is challenged in court, the party invoking it must be able to show that it was impossible to predict the actual damage at the time the deal was struck and that the agreed amount was a reasonable estimate. The *right of offset* (seen on page 82) is a related tactic. It's like having a built-in discount in your deal, to cover the other side's partial performance.

If you just bought a business, you won't want the former owner out there stealing back his or her customers. Include in your contract a *covenant not to compete*, the owner's promise not to compete with your business for an agreed period in an agreed area. Like liquidated damages, the clause has to be reasonable in scope or it won't hold up in court. By the way, another way to avoid this kind of competition is to keep the former owner on your payroll as a consultant for a set period of time. Some states may allow you to include a covenant not to compete in your agreements with key employees to prevent them from working for your archrivals. In other states, such clauses are unenforceable.

A courtroom is not the only place to settle the score. That's why more and more are turning to *arbitration, mediation,* and other forms of *alternative dispute resolution* (**ADR**) to avoid the cost and delays of the most advanced legal system the world has ever known. Chapter 9 (see pages 202–14) explores the pros and cons of **ADR** at length. The parties can agree to resolve future disputes with **ADR** by including clauses to such effect in their contract.

Unfortunately, boilerplate isn't much help when it comes to bankruptcy. Although from time to time you'll see language that automatically ends a deal if one side goes belly-up, those clauses may not survive in bankruptcy court. Those courts have broad powers, including the power to assume (hold onto) or reject *executory contracts,* contracts on which each side still has some outstanding obligations. So, depending on what's good for the bankrupt, the judge can look at a contract and take it or leave it. Due diligence, money up front, and/or solid security agreements are your best defense against shaky financials.

Finally, there's no reason you can't customize your own remedies. Murphy taught us well: Things always go wrong. So mix, match, and be creative. A heart-to-heart at the contract stage about what would be fair if things go wrong (before everyone's mad) will make things far less unpleasant when and if they do.

War Games: Getting a Leg Up at Trial

Many boilerplate provisions are designed to give one side superior firepower in the event of litigation. Here's the standard arsenal:

Service of process is a fancy term for the formal notice you owe the other side before you haul them into court. The rules are technical and bear directly on a court's jurisdiction, or legal right to decide a case. So if your adversary is the type to hide under the covers while the process server rings the doorbell, you may have a problem. A service of process clause designates a ready who and how for service, such as the other side's longtime attorney by mail, and gets your lawsuit off on the right foot.

When one side is from Maine, the other is from Arizona, and they're building in Iowa with materials from Alaska, where do you sue? Although judges don't always respect these, a *choice of forum* clause sets out which court the parties agree to use, and a *choice of law* clause specifies which state's law will apply. When used effectively, these clauses start you off with the court and body of law most favorable to you.

An *attorneys' fees* clause makes the loser of a lawsuit responsible for the winner's legal fees, as well as its own. There's something innately decent about this, and, in fact, in the English system, it's the law. In the United States, attorneys' fees are awarded by statute only some of the time. Of course, if you're the one more likely to get sued and to lose, don't add this clause to your contract.

Our law still sustains the traditional English distinction between actions *at law* and *in equity*. The former are simply lawsuits for damages (money); the latter ask the court do something fairer when money just won't cut it. An *injunction*, the court's ordering someone not to do something, is one kind of equitable relief. Others include the *rescission*, or *reformation* of a contract, or even *specific performance*: a court's forcing a party to go through with the deal. With this in mind, clever deal makers try to control *equitable remedies* by getting their opponents to either waive or agree to specific ones from the get-go. Sometimes it's permissible, other times it's presumptuous, but generally you've got nothing to lose by trying. For instance, a record company will make each artist: (1) acknowledge its right to stop the artist from recording for another label while that artist is under contract to it; and (2) waive his or her right to stop the record company from selling the star's records, regardless of the circumstances. You may also

---

SOME RIGHTS YOU CANNOT WAIVE

- constitutional rights
- all remedies
- statute of limitations
- the right to attack a contract for fraud or duress
- the right to a discharge of a debt in bankruptcy
- the defenses created by usury laws
- all rights to counterclaim or set off in a lawsuit
- rights in the collateral you put up (you may not agree that a creditor may treat collateral any way it wants, keep it as long as it wants, or enter to repossess it whenever it wants)
- rights in insurance claims (i.e., that a creditor may settle claims against a debtor's insurer)

Fig. 4.6

run into a *severability* provision, which provides that if one part of a contract is held illegal or unenforceable, the rest of it will still stand.

Waiver, which we touched on, is the release of some right or privilege. It's a great way to stack the deck. Your fantasy boilerplate will cement in every right you may, ought, should, could, or would have, while having your opponent waive all equitable remedies, trial by jury, and every possible legal defense. A lot is possible here, but before you get carried away, know that even if you can get the other side to go for it, a court won't honor every waiver you dream up; see figure 4.6. A clause in which one side acknowledges that they were represented by an attorney, or knowingly waived that right, can help establish that party's capacity and more equal bargaining power.

GUARDING THE FAMILY JEWELS: PROTECTING YOUR ASSETS

> As one gets older, litigation replaces sex.
>
> —Gore Vidal

Call him *Homo litigious*, for twentieth-century American man loves to litigate. And the more deals you make, the greater your chances of being sued. It's been estimated that in the U.S. a claim is filed every thirty seconds. Whether the lawsuit is legit or not, you must defend, at your cost, on your time, and regardless of how petty and aggravating it all is. Thus, enter the specialization euphemistically known as *asset protection*. A unique blend of probate, bankruptcy, and corporate law, a solid asset-protection plan will shield a deal maker's assets, making it either impossible or unbelievably time-consuming and expensive for anyone to get them.

Far more respectable today, asset protection was born from the work done to help financial crooks hide their money, legally. So before we start, consider this: Although you may legally outwit your creditors, is it ethical to make yourself judgment-proof against valid claims? Of course not. But who's to say which claims are just: a judge? a jury? your superego? With all the frivolous claims and absurd jury awards, shouldn't *you* be the one to decide which claims you'll honor? Anyway, that's the basic sales pitch. If you feel uncomfortable with some of what follows, you're not alone. Still, every deal maker should be aware of these techniques even if he or she never intends to use them. Because if the other side seems to know every trick in the book, beware!

The Wrong Way to Be a Deadbeat: Fraudulent Conveyances

No, you can't just wait till the last second and put everything in your wife's or best friend's name. If you transfer property with actual intent to "delay, hinder, or defraud" your creditors you've engaged in a *fraudulent conveyance*, which in its more egregious forms is criminal. Our law, in this regard, dates back to the 1571 English Statute of Elizabeth; today it's part of the federal bankruptcy code as well as all state codes.

Over the last four hundred years the main enhancement to fraudulent conveyance law has involved the meaning of "actual intent." Certainly, if you transferred property without making a fair exchange at a time when you should have known you were going bust, a court may find either that your intent was obvious or insignificant, in that your actions speak for themselves. The latter is sometimes referred to as "constructive" fraudulent conveyance. To fill in the gaps, fraudulent conveyance law also sets out so-called *badges of fraud*, which are other factors it'll use to determine actual intent:

- Transfers made secretly or in haste
- Intrafamily transfers
- Transfers to an "insider," such as a dummy corporation under the debtor's control
- Transfer of substantially all of the debtor's property
- Transfers made while the debtor was in litigation or in anticipation of litigation
- Transfers in which the debtor remains in control of property
- Concealment or removal of assets
- Transfers occurring shortly before or after a substantial debt was incurred
- A lien given by the debtor to a third party who then transferred the assets to an insider
- Transfers outside the ordinary course of business

Shielding Your Assets: Essentials

Thus, fraudulent conveyance is *the* issue in asset protection. Making sure you get as few of the badges of fraud pinned on you is critical. So, if you're going to play hide-the-money, at the very least . . .

1. *Have a solid reason that's not related to hindering creditors.* For instance:
- income tax planning (like shifting income to children to take advantage of lower tax rates)
- estate planning
- marital planning (prenuptial, postnuptial, or divorce settlements)
- business planning (such as dividing your business among several corporations for financing purposes)
- taking advantage of statutory exemptions, such as the homestead (see below)

2. *Do it early.* Do it before you need to, well in advance of any claims. In many states a court can reach back four or even six years to invalidate a fraudulent conveyance. If your transfers took place early enough you may completely avoid the reach of these statutes.

3. *Do it a little at a time.* Not only does it attract less attention, but it's hard to prove you were obstructing creditors if a transfer was relatively small in relation to your total net worth. Scatter your wealth.

4. *Don't do it all.* If you leave your creditors something, eventually they'll be more likely to go away.

5. *Make everything look arms-length.*
- Don't transfer to relatives or close business associates.
- Get appraisals to establish value.
- Make sure the person you're transferring to has their own attorney.
- Don't look like you're still in control of the property (for example, continuing to live in the house or to manage the business you just sold).
- Make sure you can justify an exchange as fair.

6. *Layer or combine strategies.* By the time you finish reading this section, you'll know many techniques. Combine them for greater protection.

7. *Only pick transferees you really trust.* They may have to defend your dealings in open court.

8. *Tie up your assets.* The more liens, options, or encumbrances your assets are subject to, the less anyone will want them. This ties into the recommendations in "Keep a Low Profile" (see below). The less you seem to own, the better.

Protecting Your Assets: The Strategies

Here's the basic menu. Some strategies are more effective. Some are more expensive. Some are more complicated. And most require a good attorney.

Run
When creditors knock on your front door, duck out the back . . . preferably to another state. In its low-rent form this tack is ludicrous, patently fraudulent, ineffective (since it's pretty easy for a creditor to track you down), and impractical (unless you think you're Richard Kimble). On the other hand, moving your assets to another state can be quite effective if you take advantage of liberal homestead and other exemptions (see below).

Renegotiate
If your deal isn't working out, try to cut a new one. Stay in touch with your creditors. To a large extent your interests are identical: You want to pay and they want to get paid. And of course, partial payment is

better than none. Bankruptcy lawyers devise incredibly creative ways to "work it out." Also, see pages 202–203 in Chapter 9.

Keep a Low Profile

If you look like a deep pocket, people will treat you like one. It's not so much your suits, car, or jewelry as your control over what others can learn about what you own. Don't forget the computer moles we met in Step 3. Secrecy is a theme that runs through asset protection. If your assets are titled so that they're impossible to trace back to you, your fortress will stand intact. Here are some possibilities:

• *If you can, deal in cash.* It's more difficult to trace. Just keep your eye on current reporting requirements (as of this writing, banks are required to report cash transactions of $10,000 and over).

• *Consider bearer investments.* They require a little know-how when it comes to buying and selling, but gold, jewelry, stamps, and other collectibles can shelter substantial wealth. Warning: If you insure them, you're creating a paper trail.

• *Scatter your assets.* They're harder to track that way.

• *Choose a team who'll keep your confidence.* Lawyers are automatically bound by the attorney-client privilege. With others, like bankers and accountants, you may have to be more explicit.

• *Be stingy with information.* Sometimes you have little choice, but as we saw in Step 3, it's amazing what others can learn about you through public and other records. Brag about what you own on an insurance or loan application and you may live to regret it.

• *Consider offshore bank accounts.* Many keep the bulk of their funds in the Bahamas, the Cayman Islands, or Switzerland. The upside is their financial privacy. In some jurisdictions, you can even charter your own bank. The downside is that accounts may pay low interest or be inconvenient, uninsured, or easily affected by political instability.

• *Get a private post office box.* Make sure it's not traceable to you.

• *Keep property out of your name and technical control.* Use trusts, corporations, and limited partnerships . . . details to follow.

• *Don't put your creditors in touch with each other.* Keep the lines of communication open, but don't help them team up on you.

Declare Bankruptcy

Of course, they wouldn't call it going belly-up if it didn't sound like unconditional surrender. Ostensibly, bankruptcy has two purposes: (1) to give debtors a fresh start, and (2) to make sure creditors are treated fairly. Once a petition is filed, creditors are essentially *stayed*, or stopped from doing anything to collect, until a special bankruptcy court sorts things out. But as Kevin Delaney suggests in his book *Strategic Bankruptcy*, bankruptcy is becoming, more and more, not a disgraceful end of the line or stigmatized rehabilitation but another strategy for the shrewd deal maker. Consider Johns-Manville's filing in 1982, which avoided asbestos claims, or Continental Airlines' filing in 1983, which was a union buster, or Texaco's 1987 filing, which avoided a $10 billion judgment to Pennzoil . . . when Texaco had $37 billion in assets!

In many cases, bankruptcy may help you keep what's yours. It comes in three basic flavors:

• *Chapter 7*, with certain exceptions, will eliminate your debts by liquidating your *nonexempt* assets (see below). Sometimes called *straight bankruptcy*, it's the most popular, available to corporations and individuals whether or not they're engaged in a business. It's truly a fresh start.

• *Chapter 11* allows a debtor to keep their assets, reorganize their business, and arrange a repayment plan with creditors, all under the watchful eye of the court. Like Chapter 7, it's also available to corporations and individuals.

• *Chapter 13*, the *wage-earner* plan, is a lot like Chapter 11, allowing those who qualify (individuals with less than $250,000 in unsecured debt and $750,000 in secured debt) to keep their assets while straightening out their debts.

Know that certain debts generally are not dischargeable in bankruptcy: among them, taxes, child support, alimony, certain student loans, criminal fines and penalties, monies owed for willful or malicious injury, debts you didn't list on your filing, and debts involving fraud. Also, bankruptcy courts have broad powers; even if a debt is outside one of these categories, if the court thinks it would be unfair to let you off the hook, given the circumstances, it won't.

As with most things in life, timing is critical. For example, a bankruptcy court can reach back one year from the date of filing to invalidate a fraudulent transfer, ninety days to rectify a *preference* (favored treatment of one or more creditors over others), and sixty days to make you return luxury items and cash advances on a credit card over $1,000. Factor in cash flow and you can see why debtors pick the date they file with great precision.

Certainly, whenever solvency is an issue, bankruptcy is a trapdoor waiting to be sprung, and this short tour merely outlines a few of the most basic considerations. Remember, a clever debtor can exploit the Bankruptcy Code to avoid creditors and thereby continue doing business as usual. So, as I've said before, do diligence (Step 3), use your street smarts (pages 81–89), and if collateral is involved, take first-priority security interests wherever you can.

Use Homestead and Other Exemptions

Former Texas governor John Connolly emerged from bankruptcy a multimillionaire! He did it by using an *exemption*, a law that declares certain property off-limits to creditors. Both Florida and Texas have huge *homestead* exemptions: In Texas, anything you build on one urban acre or 200 rural acres, and in Florida, anything built on one-half of an urban acre or 160 rural acres, is generally exempt from claims of creditors.

Exemptions vary dramatically from state to state. Many are small, protecting property of a certain type (like the family Bible, the family rifle, or health aids); of a certain value (say, personal property up to $5,000); or of a certain type and value (for example, tools of the trade worth not more than $2,500). Depending on the state, significant exemptions may be available for pension plans, life insurance policies, and annuities.

As you'd expect, there are exceptions to exemptions. For example, to claim a homestead, filings are sometimes required. Also, exemptions may not protect you from the IRS or your own intentional bad acts. If you intend to arrange your assets to take advantage of exemptions, investigate and plan carefully.

Till Debt Do Us Part

It must be a cold-blooded couple indeed who would stage a friendly divorce just to frustrate creditors! Yet prenuptial, postnuptial, and divorce settlement agreements all affect the ownership of assets and, ultimately, what and whether a creditor can collect from which spouse. Thus, a well-planned transfer of property into the name of the less vulnerable spouse makes sense, if the other doesn't mind losing legal control of that asset.

Choosing the Right Entity: Part 1

Here we'll see how corporations, limited partnerships, and trusts can be used specifically to shield assets. Later, in Chapter 7, we'll revisit the corporation and limited partnership as ways to structure the relationship among those working on the same side of a deal.

The Corporation: The Pros. A fictitious entity separate from its owner and managers, a *corporation* can do business in its own name like a real person. However, its shareholders are liable only to the extent of their investment.

Due to its familiarity and limited-liability feature, the corporation is the entity of choice among defensive deal makers. By using several corporations, you can insulate each part of a business from the others. Your real estate, equipment, and patents can each be owned by a different one. By exploiting the technicalities of corporate law, like assessments and transfer restrictions on shares of stock, shareholder proxies, or cleverly drafted articles of incorporation, bylaws, and shareholder's agreements, you can cement your control, effectively making your stock worthless to a creditor. By mortgaging corporate assets to the hilt you turn a "deep pocket" into "scorched earth," leaving little equity for the taking. And by selecting the state of incorporation, you choose the law that's best for you. Delaware is often used for large, publicly held corporations because its laws are well understood and quite protective of officers, directors, and shareholders. Nevada is widely regarded as tops for privately held corporations; among its many advantages are favorable tax laws and minimal reporting requirements. For example, the names of shareholders of a Nevada corporation need not be a matter of public record.

The Corporation: The Cons. On the other hand, a corporation is no magic shield. It won't protect a promoter who has misled investors. It grants no immunity from certain environmental liabilities, such as the Superfund. Its directors may still be liable for their own negligence, insider loans, improper dividends, and violations of tax, securities, corporate, civil rights, or antitrust laws. And if you were required to give a personal guaranty, as is often the case with new corporations or ones with few assets, limited liability is limited indeed.

Piercing the Corporate Veil. Finally, there are times when courts will disregard a corporation and visit on its shareholders the sins of the entity. *Piercing the corporate veil* has been called the most litigated and least understood issue in corporate law. In an empirical study for the *Cornell Law Review*, Professor Robert B. Thompson writes that it's practically impossible to lay down hard-and-fast rules for how a court will act. Yet 40 percent of reported cases result in piercing. Fraud, undercapitalization, and a lack of separateness seem to be the top three no-no's. In any event, the more a corporation looks like a flimsy little alter ego, the more likely it'll be disregarded and its shareholders held personally liable. Check out figure 4.7 for some practical advice on how to avoid this problem.

DON'T LET A COURT SET ASIDE YOUR CORPORATION

- Don't operate as a corporation until the incorporation and financing are complete.
- Avoid personal guaranties; don't cosign the corporation's loans.
- With third parties, be clear that you're doing business as a corporation.
- The more shareholders, the better.
- Don't use your corporation to evade the law or avoid contractual obligations.
- Observe formalities.
  - Keep your books in good shape.
  - Issue stock.
  - Hold annual shareholders' and directors' meetings. Take minutes. Record formal resolutions and official acts.
  - File all required annual reports.
  - Sign all contracts as an officer of and in the name of the corporation, not your own. Don't sign your name followed by "dba" ("doing business as").
  - Don't commingle corporate and individual funds.
- Make sure your corporation is adequately funded: A 4 or 5 to 1 debt to equity ratio is a rule of thumb sometimes given.
- Make sure you have enough liability insurance.

Fig. 4.7

The Limited Partnership

A *limited partnership* is a partnership consisting of one or more general partners, who run the business and are liable for all of its debts, and one or more limited, or silent, partners, who, like corporate shareholders, are liable for what they put in. General and limited partners can be individuals or other entities, like corporations.

Limited partners have limited liability, unless they start managing the enterprise and acting like general partners. The general partner controls the enterprise's assets and, among other things, decides if and when the limiteds get profits. Thus, the lucky creditor that gets a *charging order* against a limited partner and is allowed to seize a limited partner's interest may get little indeed: An interest in an enterprise that guarantees no profits, grants no say in the business, and consequently has little market value. Limited partners may wait indefinitely for a payout as a crafty general partner quietly rearranges assets to avoid distributions. Depending on how it's set up, that creditor may even have to pay taxes on his or her profits, before receiving one cent!

Trusts

A *trust* is created when one person holds property for another's benefit. Trusts are essential in estate and tax planning and for managing the assets of minors and incompetents. Although they're rarely the business entity of choice today, when it comes to protecting what's yours, they're the Rolls-Royce of asset-protection vehicles. Once you transfer an asset into a trust, technically you no longer own it. Ergo, your creditors can't touch it.

Naturally, setting up a trust must be done correctly. A revocable trust does you little good. Basically, courts see creditors as standing in your shoes; if you can get the asset, so can they. As always, watch out for fraudulent conveyances, preferences, and other legal snags. Generally, the less control you have over the trust on paper, the greater your protection. As a practical matter, your informal relationship with your carefully chosen trustee will make you the de facto manager. You can often keep the beneficiaries of a trust a secret. Thus, even a revocable trust may be useful, if your creditors can't link it to you.

If you set up a trust offshore (for example, in the Cook or Cayman Islands), you turn your asset-protection plan into a work of art. To the normal benefits of the trust, add debtor-friendly foreign laws (which often include fewer reporting requirements, shorter statutes of limitations, favorable fraudulent conveyance laws, and nonrecognition of U.S. judgments and consequently the need to try cases from scratch), plus the expense of litigating across international borders. Sprinkle your assets through half a dozen jurisdictions, mix in a few corporations and limited partnerships, and now you're really playing in the majors. By the way, this game's for high rollers only. Budget your initial legal fees and other costs at $10,000 to $25,000 per trust.

END GAME: W. C. FIELDS AND THE RISK OF MANAGING RISK

> The policy of being too cautious is the
> greatest risk of all.
>
> —Jawaharlal Nehru

Yes, there are a thousand ways your deal can go down the tubes. But if you obsess about each risk, you'll never make the Forbes 400. You can't manage them all, nor should you. So take an active attitude and choose your risks wisely. Learn from W. C. Fields. In one of his famous saloon scenes we observe the crafty comic studying his poker hand for a long time. A man asks, "Mr. Fields, is this a game of chance?" Fields pauses, then replies, "Not the way I play it!"

5

STEP 5:

NEGOTIATE

Ultimatum, n. . . . A last demand before
resorting to concessions.
                    —Ambrose Bierce, *The Devil's Dictionary*

Of all six steps, negotiation is the most exciting. Until now we've just been armchair generals—analyzing, organizing, scrutinizing, theorizing, and strategizing. Now it's time to engage in that most ancient and universal of business activities: negotiation. To many, negotiation is the quintessence of deal making. To me, it's merely a part, the customizing of a deal to each side's satisfaction. But all agree that negotiation is what makes a deal a reality.

KNOWING WHEN TO WALK AWAY

The more I compare the popular primers on negotiation to my own experience, the more I reject absolute rules. "Never make the first offer." "Never give something for nothing." "Never let on that you don't know." These may sound like bargaining bedrock, but real life teaches that exceptions swallow the rules. In negotiation, there are no commandments. Yet if there's one truth that approaches an absolute, it's this: Set your bottom line before you negotiate. If you can't negotiate a deal at least as good, walk away.

In a simple deal, stick to an absolute number or demand. This approach may be rigid, but it's also the easiest and safest. In a more complicated deal, take a tip from Roger Fisher, William Ury, and Bruce Patton, the authors of *Getting to Yes*. Consider your "BATNA," your Best Alternative To a Negotiated Agreement. In other words, before you close any deal, ask yourself whether you've got a better option. If you don't, sign. If you do, walk. BATNA offers flexibility and encourages creative problem solving. However, it does force you to reevaluate your bottom line in the heat of battle, when you may not be your clearest.

Negotiation is stressful. Endless talks, manipulative opponents, labyrinthine issues, and concocted crises, whipped up with your own hopes and insecurities, can and will impair your judgment. As you negotiate, you may get confused, anxious, tongue-tied, or simply out-witted. But if you know when to say no, you'll never get hurt.

LEARNING YOUR OPPONENT

> I have studied the enemy all my life. I have read the memoirs of his generals and his leaders. I have even read his philosophers and listened to his music. I have studied in detail the account of every damned one of his battles. I know exactly how he will react under any given set of circumstances, and he hasn't the slightest idea of what I'm going to do. So when the time comes, I'm going to whip the hell out of him.
>
> —General George S. Patton

Patton's combative tone is inappropriate for most negotiations, but his obsession with probing inquiry is not. If you don't know who you're up against, you may shake on a deal and walk away missing a few fingers.

In Step 3 we learned how to smoke out frauds, cons, and scams while asking a threshold question: "Should we do this deal?" Now you know you'd like to do business, but you need to learn more about your opponent *as a negotiator*, because if you know what to expect when you sit down to bargain, you will dramatically enhance your ability to get what you want. Here are five key questions to ask before beginning a negotiation:

Who's Got the Upper Hand?

Few negotiations take place between evenly seated players. Study figure 5.1. How do you stack up against your opponent? Be honest with

FIGURE IT OUT: WHO'S GOT THE CLOUT?

Which side has more power?
. . . who's bigger?
. . . who's got greater resources?
. . . who's got more outside influence?
. . . who's got more knowledgeable players?
. . . who can help the other more?
. . . who can hurt the other more?
. . . who's more willing to use power?

Which side is better at negotiation?
. . . who's got more experience?
. . . who's more organized?
. . . who's quicker on their feet?
. . . who's sharper?
. . . who's smoother?
. . . who's tougher?
. . . who's more intimidating?
. . . who can cop the best attitude?

Which side has momentum?
. . . who's got more info?
. . . who's more focused on the deal?
. . . who's got more logical arguments?
. . . who's got more expertise?
. . . who's got industry custom on their side?
. . . who's got the fairer arguments?
. . . who knows more about the other?
. . . who's willing to take more risks?
. . . who likes who more?

Which side wants the deal more?
. . . who needs the deal more?
. . . who likes the deal more?
. . . who's invested more in the deal?
. . . who's giving the deal more attention?
. . . who's more committed?
. . . who's pushing the deal forward?
. . . who's got more important people working on the deal?
. . . who's more responsive?
. . . who's getting stressed out more?
. . . who has better alternatives?

Fig. 5.1

yourself. By assessing the other side's strengths and weaknesses, you also assess your own. This is where strategy starts. Never forget that power, in whatever form, is *the* key player in a negotiation. As you negotiate, revisit figure 5.1 periodically to reassess who's got the upper hand.

Who's the *Real* Decision Maker?

There's no point closing a deal with the wrong person. It's up to you to learn who's really calling the shots. Never assume you're dealing with the right person. Entrepreneurs have partners, salespeople have supervisors, husbands and wives have each other. Is the person you're negotiating with a pawn, bishop, or rook, or the king himself? If you're negotiating with a group that has no clear leader, sell to the members who want the deal most.

Large organizations are a special problem. Who hasn't sealed a deal with George Jetson only to have it nixed by Mr. Spacely? Before you get in too deep, do "recon" on Spacely Sprockets. Who does Jetson report to? How far can he go on his own? What's the procedure for getting Spacely's O.K.? Know titles, but don't let them intimidate or fool you. An assistant manager at one outfit may have more power than a senior vice president at another. Uncover the true pecking order by working your business grapevine, especially any contacts you may have inside a company. Don't be afraid to ask the person you're dealing with directly about their authority. Find out what you can do to move things along. And if your George needs to go up the ladder for approval, make him promise to go to bat for you.

What's Negotiable and What's Not?

According to the ancient military genius Sun Tzu, "he who knows when he can fight and when he cannot will be victorious." Businesses often establish uniform policies to help them run smoothly, policies that, for good reason, are considered nonnegotiable. So be realistic. A large company isn't likely to retool its accounting system, product line, or management structure for anyone. However, at other times, declaring an issue nonnegotiable is just another way to steamroll you.

Knowing when and how hard to push is tricky. Consider your leverage, industry custom, how difficult and costly it would be for the other side to accommodate you, and whether they can live with the precedent. Once again, work your business network. Your best sources of information either are inside the company or have a lot of experience negotiating against it.

What Do They Really Want?

This may sound trite. "Emptor emit quam minimo potest, venditor vendit quam maximo potest" or, The buyer buys for as little as possible, the seller sells for as much as possible. But consider this often-told anecdote:

> Two kids squabble over the last orange in the fridge. Their father hears the ruckus, enters the kitchen, and without a word assumes the solution: He slices the fruit in equal halves and gives one to each child. Yet no one is happy. Why? Because one kid wanted to eat the pulp, and the other just needed the rind to bake!

Don't jump to conclusions about what the other side really wants. Try to uncover their underlying interests. Revisit the sections "Personal Needs" on pages 7–8 and "Questions and Answers" on pages 49–53. What you learn may not only surprise you but pave the way for an easy solution. Often differences are what make agreements possible. Why settle for either/or when you can have win/win?

Of course there are times when even your opponents won't know what drives them. As every ad executive and Freudian knows, people are not rational. Some people live to pound the table, scream foul, and storm out. Others need to be coddled, stroked, and spoon-fed. Everyone is at least a little neurotic, and we all bring our quirks to the bargaining table. The great financier Andre Mayer once said that "the merger business is 10 percent analysis and 90 percent psychoanalysis."

How Does the Other Side Negotiate?

Specifically, how will your opponent's level of experience, gender, and cultural background affect your negotiation?

How Experienced Are They?
For starters, you might think a bumpkin would be a pushover and a veteran would negotiate the shirt off your back. In fact, it's often

exactly the opposite. An ace knows the ropes, can evaluate concessions, and recognize a good deal. A naive opponent's insecurity can be paralyzing. Because they're too scared to give and take they tend to stonewall you. So with beginners it's especially important to build trust and to be patient. And if your opponent is more experienced than you are, make sure you have a knowledgeable person to bounce things off.

Are They Part of an Organization?

With organizations, it's never a question of individual style. Ralph Waldo Emerson once wrote: "An institution is the lengthened shadow of one man." I believe that every company has its own negotiating personality. For example, in the music business, one of the major labels is known as the "artist's" company. Standard concessions are made without fuss, entire albums may be recorded without a signed contract, and the company is known as pleasant to negotiate with and work for. Contrast another where one vice president described his favorite cartoon: a picture of a sour-looking executive poised over a handheld buzzer attached to a huge scoreboard filled only with lightbulbs spelling out the word NO. The caption reads, "You can run it by me, but I'm pretty sure I know what the answer's going to be."

Will Gender Come into Play?

You may take strong issue, as do I, with the prevailing stereotypes about men and women's communication styles. But the fact is that individuals do communicate differently in ways often influenced by gender. Factor in these tendencies in order to improve your rapport with both sexes. I recommend the books of Deborah Tannen, especially *Talking from 9 to 5*.

There's an even deeper, more subtle aspect to gender, which comes in the form of bias. It can be as difficult to uncover our own prejudices as it can be to own them. Even the most "politically correct" among us have a few. If you don't make every effort to bring them to light, they will cloud your judgment, garble your communication, and undermine your business (and romantic) relationships. Of course, this applies to other forms of prejudice, as well.

Will Culture Clash Be a Factor?

Did you know that the Japanese have nineteen different ways to say no? In a world increasingly dominated by international, multinational, and transnational corporations, culture plays an important role in negotiation. I believe this to be true, not only when dealing with foreigners but even with second- or third-generation Americans. In any event, the literature on this subject is voluminous and fascinating, going far beyond curious questions of international etiquette.

For example, the Japanese eschew direct confrontation, preferring an exchange of information. Russians love combat; their very word for compromise is borrowed from another language. Spanish negotiators are individualistic, Koreans are team players. Nigerians prefer the spoken word, Indians the written one. Asian languages are high-context, in that one must listen keenly to inflections, body language, and what is not said. Latin American cultures are physically demonstrative. And we Americans alienate everyone with our impatience and obsession with getting things done . . . fast, fast, fast!

It behooves those who negotiate outside their culture to prepare, whether through personal sources, books, or consultants. Expertise is available on a country-by-country basis. One of my favorite general books on the subject is *Dynamics of Successful International Business Negotiations* by Robert T. Moran and William G. Stripp. By the way, always choose your translator carefully. Don't pull a Jimmy Carter. A line in one of his 1977 speeches in Poland was mistranslated as "I desire the Poles carnally."

OPENING MOVES

It is generally better to deal by . . . the mediation of a third than by a man's self. . . . Choose men of a plainer sort, that are like to do that is committed to them, and to report back again faithfully the success, than those that are cunning to contrive out of other men's business somewhat to grace themselves, and will help the matter in report for satisfaction sake. Use . . . bold men for expostulation, fair-spoken men for persuasion, crafty men for inquiry and observation. . . . Use also such as have been lucky, and prevailed before in things wherein you have employed them; for that breeds confidence and they will strive to maintain their prescription [reputation].

—Francis Bacon, "Of Negotiating"

Do It Yourself?

Written almost four hundred years ago, these words still ring true. (And what common sense for a philosopher!) Be it your lawyer, partner, spouse, or best buddy, there are great reasons to let someone else do your bidding. Negotiators help their principals stay on good terms. They're a buffer against nasty adversaries. Through them each side can test aggressive positions without committing to them. "Hey, it's not me, it's my damned 'attack dog' lawyer." A negotiator buys you time and makes the other side work harder; now they have not one but two of you to convince.

Take another look at Bacon's advice. Do you have shortcomings as a negotiator? Are you superb at bluster but light on charm? Are you persistent but volatile? Are you easily rattled by a cranky opponent? Do you get too attached to the outcome? Maybe you're just too busy. Or maybe you find all the haggling, bickering, and dickering demeaning. Nevertheless, negotiation is a fact of business life. So compensate. Pick someone to complement your strengths and check your weaknesses.

My Place or Yours?

Where should you negotiate? Every expert has a different take. Some feel the other side should come to you. You unnerve them off their turf, you cow them with your splendid surroundings, and you move faster with better access to your people. Personally, I think the home-court advantage is overrated. There are plenty of good reasons to hit the road. You put the other side at ease. You can exploit delays that come from not having access to your office. You can walk out more easily. There are similar pros and cons about telephone negotiations. Some insist on face-to-face bargaining. Conversely, many psychologists feel that vocal stress alone, unaccompanied by distracting visual cues, is the litmus test for lying. Sometimes the person placing a call has a slight edge.

Setting the Mood

Let's return to opening moves. Know that a negotiation begins long before the first words are exchanged. It starts with each side's attitude as they walk in the door . . . which is usually a little tense. You see, no matter how clever, smooth, well-prepared, and well-positioned you are, you never know exactly what will happen. Does your adversary know something you don't? Will you be outmaneuvered? Will you lose your cool or just have a lousy day? Like it or not, you bring all your insecurities right into the room with you . . . as do your opponents.

That's why it's important to begin by building trust. Start by focusing on common interests. Even natural biological enemies like landlords and tenants both seek stability, a pleasant relationship, and well-maintained premises. Establish a cooperative mood. Try to agree on some simple things first; it will make it easier to resolve the tough ones later. And of course, if you have the personal touch, use it. Life is easier when people like you.

On the other hand, no matter how reasonable you are, not every negotiation will stay cordial. The less the participants care about the long term and the more difficult the personalities, the more likely things will turn nasty. Yet this doesn't mean that one-shot deals have to be unpleasant. As my colleagues often say: "Keep your velvet gloves on as long as possible. You can always show them your iron fists later."

The First Offer

Now, at long last, we come to the first offer! Deal makers mull over their opening positions like pro golfers pacing a critical putt. Let's take these in order: who goes first and what to ask for.

Who Goes First?

Here is one of the great maxims of negotiating: "He who mentions the first number loses." Just like any other great maxim, this one's true . . . most of the time. You'll never know if you have made your best deal if you're the one putting the first number into play. The buyer might have paid more, the seller might have taken less, if you had let them go first. Are there exceptions? Certainly. Where both sides really know the marketplace, the side making the first offer defines the issues and the negotiating range, thereby gaining the upper hand. In that case, it's easier to defend one's terms than to attack another's.

There's an important corollary to the "he who mentions the first number" rule: "Never accept the first offer." Any decent opponent monitors the other side's appetite for a deal like a hawk eyes a prairie dog. The more eager you are, the more the other side will push. The more indifferent you seem, the more they'll concede. Besides, they're also asking for more than they expect to get. So even if it's an unbelievable first offer, haggle, and if you don't haggle, at least grumble, and if you don't grumble, at least keep your glee to yourself.

How Much?

Regardless of who opens, start by asking for the best terms you can justify . . . with a straight face. There are four good reasons for this twisted little ritual. First, you can't expect to conclude a negotiation without making concessions. Start far away from your bottom line and you'll have plenty to give. Second, your opponent needs to participate in the outcome. Don't deny them a good game. Besides, no one likes a take-it-or-leave-it offer. Third, by setting high goals, you're more likely to achieve them. Any motivational speaker will tell you, "Whether you think you can, or you think you can't, you're right either way." Finally, it's the way of the world.

Of course, it's one giant mixed message . . . a morality play staged in a Persian market. "I'm not going to offer 200, or even 150, so how about 125?" "I'm not going to insult you by countering with 50, or maybe 75, so here's 100, take it or leave it." Sometimes I wonder how it all got this way. Among the Ohlone Indians, for example, haggling was considered rude. They emphasized generosity and sharing, not profit. Lowball offers could only earn you a lousy reputation and prevent you from achieving favored trading status. Thus, first offers were usually accepted.

I wish we did business more like the Ohlones. But we don't. In our world business negotiation is competitive. Unless you really trust your opponent, don't start by laying your cards on the table. You're inviting them to take you under your bottom line. Ask for more than you expect. "Go high, or go home."

THE SEVEN Cs OF NEGOTIATION

> It is naught, it is naught, saith the buyer: but when he
> is gone his way, then he boasteth.
>
> —Proverbs 20:14

Now you're on the high seas with no land in sight. You know what they want, they know what you want, and you're nautical miles apart.

You must *negotiate*! So, let's navigate the seven "Cs" of negotiation. For a superb negotiator is clever, cautious, convincing, calm, constant, creative, and complete.

Be Clever

Anticipate. Negotiation is often compared to chess, and for good reason. Before a good chess player moves, they anticipate their opponent's next. Before a grand master moves, they calculate the next dozen, or more. Before you make each move, ask yourself: How will my opponent react? You'll be shocked at just how much you can predict with just this simple approach. Another great way to prepare is to actually role-play a negotiation with someone. Take one side, then the other. You'll gain tremendous insight. If you can anticipate your opponent's objection, you'll be ready with a response. Watch good pool players sometime. With each shot, they either set up their next or leave their opponent nothing.

Be Cautious

Negotiating is all about having the other side see it your way. To some, this means gift-wrapping information as attractively as possible. To others, it's an excuse to take a moral holiday, to distort, to omit, or to lie. Be cordial, be respectful, but never take anything at face value. Whether you do it directly or indirectly, question facts (investigate independently), question numbers (get specific breakdowns and run them yourself), question motives (be suspicious). In fact, you should even question the very way your opponents try to convince you. Here's what I mean:

Intellectual Dirty Tricks

There are many legitimate ways to support an argument: precedent, fairness, recognized authority, industry standard, and so on. And there are many illegitimate ways to befuddle and mentally bully someone, using sleazy logic that flies below their mental radar. Here are some examples:

1. *Analogies.* They're lovely and poetic, but they don't prove a thing. If your opponent uses one, challenge it.
2. *Unidentified sources.* Identify them, or ignore them.

3. *Citing authority.* The authority must be reliable. As ace negotiator Chester Karass says, "For every expert, there is an equal and opposite expert."

4. *Overgeneralizations.* Watch out for the words *all* and *every*. Does such a statement really apply to your situation? Is your opponent using one isolated fact to support a sweeping conclusion?

5. *Undefined terms and fuzzy language.* We all know what words like *material*, *reasonable*, and *promptly* mean. Or do we?

6. Ad hominem *arguments.* These are attacks against the person rather than the arguments.

7. *Emotionally charged words.* Bordering on outright manipulation, these could be anything from racial or sexual epithets to subtly disparaging remarks and personal insults. In any event, you'll know 'em when you "feel" 'em. See "Psychological Warfare" on page 135.

Diversions, repetition, and not answering questions directly are also part of this game. Be prepared to pin your adversary down. I know it's tough to be so unrelentingly critical, but if you let down your guard, you're asking for a sucker punch.

Secrecy

As you should be cautious of what you hear, so should you be cautious of what you say. You may not have the recipe for Coca-Cola, the formula for Play-Doh, or the eleven secret herbs and spices in Kentucky Fried Chicken, but even information as mundane as your customer list may be valuable, not to mention legally protectible as a trade secret. If possible, reveal little or nothing. If not, at least postpone disclosure until after an agreement in principle is reached. In any event, if you must spill the beans, have the other side sign a confidentiality agreement first. In its barest form it will specify what is secret and who does and doesn't get to know. However, the more valuable your secrets, the more important it is to have your lawyer prepare a comprehensive agreement that will really protect them.

Be Convincing

Persuade, persuade, persuade. Make your case with the other side. Lyman Beecher, a famous nineteenth-century preacher, called persuasion "logic on fire." Prepare your arguments thoroughly:

- have the facts at your fingertips
- find out how the other side has done it before
- research the applicable industry's custom and practice regarding the deal you're working on
- be ready to suggest objective standards (like market value, or what a court or expert would think is fair)
- if you've got the credentials, present yourself as an authority
- be ready to speak earnestly about what's fair and why

Of course, it's not only what you say but how you say it. Speak with conviction and enthusiasm. If you've got charm, pour it on. Become a perpetual student of argumentation. Consider this from Aristotle: "The fool tells me his reasons; the wise man persuades me with my own." By this time you've done so much homework, you probably know what the other side wants better than they do! Use this to make your proposals irresistible. Ask your opponent to trade places and consider things from your point of view. Because value is a key issue in any negotiation, review "Value: Will It Be Worth It?" on pages 9–14. It'll help you craft even more support for your position.

Another great way to win someone over is to never openly disagree with them. Thumb through any textbook on sales and I'm sure you'll find this dictum, along with the feel/felt/found technique, an elegant example of verbal judo. It works like this: When the other side raises an objection: (1) reassure them that you understand how they *feel*; (2) let them know that many others have *felt* the same way; and (3) conclude by telling them about the solution you and others have *found* that really works, which is your true response to their concern. It's a diplomatic way to overcome many objections.

Be Calm

"Non illegitum carborundom" or, Don't let the bastards wear you down. Unless you're able to shut down your emotions, negotiation is trying. I don't mean to sound like a pop psychologist, but you've got to take care of yourself. Opponents will push your buttons, by mistake or by design. Lose your self-control and you give away your power. Stay centered and you may actually enjoy yourself. Also, by staying calm, you'll be able to make your occasional well-timed outburst that much more effective.

The other part of keeping cool has to do with giving yourself time to think. Very few important decisions in a negotiation need to be made on the spot. Don't let yourself be pressured. You can buy time by simply asking for repetition or clarification, writing it all down, keeping quiet, telling a joke, creating a distraction, staging an interruption, or simply saying you'd like some time to think it over.

Be Constant

That is, be persistent. Perseverance is the key to success in most activities. Negotiation is no exception. The humorist Doc Blakely once said, "Success is getting up just one more time than you fall down." Often it's not about ability, luck, or leverage, just raw willpower and nerve. Hang tough. Stand your ground. Ask again and again and again. If you must move on to other issues, insist on returning to the point you must have. Don't allow yourself to be bullied or manipulated. Persist. And along with perseverance, learn patience. Here's a great example:

For four long months in the fall of 1985 Revlon's management leveraged-buyout team, led by Michel Bergerac, stymied billionaire Ron Perelman's takeover efforts. Fully aware of the traps hidden in federal securities law, Perelman and his team cooked up the "Yertle the Turtle" strategy, named after a Dr. Seuss character. "Just top every Bergerac offer by a little. Let's keep the ball in play long enough for Bergerac to commit a legal blunder." Under intense financial pressure, Perelman waited patiently. And it paid off. Bergerac dropped the ball. He tried sidestepping Perelman with a sweet deal (I'll skip the details) orchestrated by another leveraged-buyout specialist. Perelman sued, claiming the side deal prevented Revlon stockholders from getting full market value for their shares. Perelman won the suit and control of Revlon.

Let's return to Francis Bacon once more: "In all negotiations of difficulty, a man may not look to sow and reap at once; but must prepare business, and so ripen it by degrees." When the other side is holding out for what you think is no good reason, usually it's not because you haven't been persuasive. They just need time to digest. Let them have it.

Be Creative

Getting agreement on all the niggling details of even the simplest deal can tax anyone's ingenuity. Imagine how much more so when deals are complex. In these cases, creativity becomes essential; it's what separates the good negotiators from the great ones.

Take a simple demand: higher wages. Management and labor seem miles apart. Yet maybe the union would drop that demand for a one-time bonus, or a better health plan, or longer breaks, or more vacation. Or maybe management could live with increases based on merit, or seniority, or attendance. Or both sides could agree to a delayed wage hike, or to let an arbitrator decide, or to some combination of all of the above. The possibilities are as endless as the originality of the negotiators.

So when the old pat solutions aren't working, be creative. Go back to Step 1. Invite the other side's participation. Build rapport by trading ideas, constructive criticism, and alternatives. Creativity can be win/win and fun, if everyone's open to something new. I guarantee that these will be your most memorable and, hopefully, most successful negotiations.

Concessions and Conditions

When it comes to creative negotiation, there are two tools every deal maker must master: the *concession* and the *condition*. Simply put, a concession is what you give, and a condition is what you get. Grammatically speaking, a condition is the "if" clause; a concession is the "then." "If you pay now, then I'll knock off 15 percent." "If you finish by Tuesday, then you get a bonus." "If you'll give me a bigger slice of the profits later, then I'll take less cash now." Clever use of the concession and the condition is the trademark of the inventive deal maker.

Each concession involves a little minideal. You give in order to get. Even seemingly unilateral concessions create tacit obligations, jump-start talks, and generate goodwill, all of which are benefits to you. So before you give, always consider what you'll get. And if you choose to cut a really hard bargain, don't just go tit for tat. Use each "give" to get as much as possible. Besides, being stingy with your concessions will wear the other side down and discourage additional demands.

On the other hand, the condition is not only the better half of any exchange, since it's what you get, but a great way to control the negotiation as a whole. In this way it's even more powerful than the concession. It has virtually unlimited applications. Here are just a few ideas:

• *Refuse to make any concessions until you know all the demands.* This is a most effective use of the condition. Make it part of your standard repertoire. If you don't, you're bargaining on quicksand. Just when you think you're done, up comes yet one more demand, and another, and another, and another.

• *Negotiate how you'll negotiate.* Call this a "meta-negotiation." Condition your very participation on the time, place, number of participants, agenda, or similar conditions, cleverly stacking the deck in your favor. Remember the Vietnam peace talks? Given upcoming presidential elections, the North Vietnamese gained tremendous power by delaying discussion over more substantive issues with endless bickering over the shape of the bargaining table.

• *Condition your agreement on the approval of a "higher authority."* It buys you time to think or regroup, and that authority can be anybody . . . your boss, your wife, your partner, or even your dog. We've seen this before in "Who's the *Real* Decision Maker?" (page 121) and we'll learn more about the higher authority soon in "Dirty Tricks."

• *Condition all your concessions on each other.* This is sometimes called a package deal and gives your opponent a strong incentive to close. After all, one more demand and you may revoke everything. For example, trading in a car is often three deals in one: the deal for your old car, the deal for your new car, and the financing deal. To make a good deal overall, you must make a good deal on each one. So condition your agreement on each individual deal on your agreement to the other two.

Deadlock

Creativity is usually the key to breaking through an impasse. Start by rekindling your rapport with the other side. If there are some easy points outstanding, settle those first and save the sticky ones for later. Then, with fresh eyes, look to change something about the deal itself: the terms, the time periods, the payment schedules, the apportionment of risk, or some other element. See figure 5.2 for more ideas. If you refocus on underlying concerns and engage your creativity, there's a good chance a solution will emerge.

17 WAYS TO BUST A DEADLOCK

1. Brainstorm creative alternatives.
2. Look for an outside standard or precedent.
3. Go off the record.
4. Have the principals work it out.
5. Take a break.
6. Get a mediator or arbitrator.
7. Try a procedural solution (e.g., draw lots; flip a coin; one cuts, the other chooses).
8. Appeal to someone with more authority.
9. Set a time limit.
10. Speed up.
11. Slow down.
12. Crack a joke.
13. Set up a meeting or a conference call.
14. Change the negotiators.
15. Spend more time studying the problem.
16. Bring in an expert.
17. Do nothing.

Fig. 5.2

Be Complete

You need stamina to negotiate. Don't get lazy. Review your checklist. Don't assume an important issue will work itself out tomorrow just because you don't feel like dealing with it today. Be thorough and, above all, read the next chapter. You're not done until you get everything in writing.

DIRTY TRICKS

> Let every eye negotiate for itself
> And trust no agent.
> —Shakespeare, *Much Ado About Nothing*

By now it's obvious: Negotiation is a game, albeit a serious one. Some players are good sports; others are not. Some rely on their ability to persist and persuade, others on their ability to deceive and exploit. Unfortunately, manipulators and swindlers are frequent guests at the bargaining table. So be wary and be wise.

What follows is a laundry list of classic gambits. Depending on the tactic and the context, they range from kind of acceptable to offensive to downright sleazy. Find your own comfort level. As you read, I'm sure you'll be able to tell where I stand.

Psychological Warfare

"Do unto others before they do unto you." Welcome to the "rape and pillage" school of negotiation, negotiation–*cum*–psychological warfare.

You don't have to be the brightest candle on the birthday cake to recognize these tactics. Bluster, insults, intractable positions, whining, lecturing, constant interruptions, yelling, and phony deadlines will set your teeth on edge. But watch out for the sneak attack. One opponent fatigues you with all-night talks in inhospitable surroundings. Another dulls you with wine and rich meals before scrambling information and switching negotiators. Before important negotiations, the legendary lawyer Clarence Darrow used to insert a thin wire lengthwise through his cigar. As it slowly smoldered down to a butt, his adversaries would be driven to distraction wondering why the ash didn't fall. In any event, don't underestimate these tactics. They work. You'll give away the store just to get it over with. And what's worse is that you've rewarded the other side for its rudeness, encouraging them to do it all over again.

So what do you do? First, reconsider getting into bed with this adversary. Shabby treatment this early on is not a good sign. If you decide to continue, stay calm (one of the seven Cs of negotiation). Protest the treatment if you like, but don't fight fire with fire; it's counterproductive. Ignore the histrionics, the blame game, the manipulations, and the personal attacks. Remain cooperative and optimistic. If you must, let them vent, or mirror their feelings or massage their egos. But in any event, keep bringing the other side back again and again to a rational discussion of the issues.

The Higher Authority

Early in the movie *Out of Africa*, the character played by Meryl Streep, Karen, tries to convince a sick Kikiyu boy, named Kamante, to go to the hospital:

> KAREN: This leg is very sick; it should go to the hospital.
>
> KAMANTE (grave): This leg may be foolish. It may think not to go to the hospital.
>
> KAREN: . . . If you will take this foolish leg to the hospital, and keep it there until it is strong, I will think that you are wise and have done a good thing. Such a wise man as that I would want to work in my house, for wages.
>
> KAMANTE: How much wages would come to such a wise man as that?
>
> KAREN: More wages than come at tending goats.
>
> KAMANTE (considers this): I will talk to this leg then.

Kamante has put a new spin on the doctrine of higher authority. He's got his sick leg calling the shots! Remember this drill? Your opponent negotiates but won't fully commit until checking with someone else first. Accept it stoically when there are legitimate chains of command. Protest it when used to delay, obstruct, or grind you down by bringing in new, or imaginary, players to rework settled points. And call it bogus when staged as the infamous good cop, bad cop routine.

Good Cop, Bad Cop

It goes something like this: During interrogation Bad Cop brutalizes Suspect. Suspect won't talk. Exit Bad Cop. Enter Good Cop. Good Cop offers Suspect a cigarette. "Boy, oh boy," says Good Cop, "that Bad Cop is one tough cookie." Suspect starts to relax. Maybe Good Cop's on his side. Good Cop throws out a little bait: "Hey, maybe I can get him to go a little easy on you." Suspect weakens. Suspect starts to sing.

This isn't just grade B film noir. It happens every day. You strike a deal with the salesman for the car of your dreams. Then the floor manager torpedoes it. The home seller's wife pulls you aside: "Oh, I know my husband's a bear. Can't you raise your offer just a tad?" That snotty little suit moans about how the board of directors has his hands tied.

Never forget that the good cop and the bad cop are one unit. Negotiate *directly* with the bad cop, or with the two of them together to eliminate the "shield" they give each other. If you're shrewd and a little lucky, you can even play them off each other. However, veteran negotiator Herb Cohen has the best advice: "A tactic perceived is no tactic." Tell them, nicely, that you're onto them. Good cop, bad cop is such a cheesy little ploy. Once you've called them on it, they're likely to be too embarrassed to continue.

The Meaningless Concession

A criminal pleads with the judge about his cruel punishment: two consecutive life sentences. The judge relents, slicing the sentence in half. This is a meaningless concession. In negotiation, it goes like this: You pick out demands that are really important to the other side but easy for you to accommodate. Then you trade your easy gives for their significant concessions. The trick is in making the other side believe that you're really going out of your way for them. It's a textbook gambit. Of course, it also works in reverse. So the next time your opponent claims they're bending over backward, ask yourself: "When is a concession not a concession?"

Straw Men, Red Herrings, and Decoys

These are second cousins to the meaningless concession. They all mean the same thing. You distract your opponent with a staged hubbub around some trivial or unrealistic demand. Later you exchange it for something worthwhile. As with the meaningless concession, a skeptical attitude is your best defense.

Nibbling

A nibble is that last itty-bitty concession the other side requests, just before you shake on it. "That includes delivery, doesn't it?" the customer inquires with doelike innocence. The salesperson types up your order and murmurs, "By the way, the deluxe carrying case is extra." It's a nice ploy for two reasons. First, it's just a nibble, not a whole bite. Second, the other side's defenses are down. In their minds, the deal is closed and they don't want to renegotiate, so they give in. When you're up against a skilled nibbler, you can insist on sticking to the agreement, you can nibble right back, or you can shame them into submission: "Haven't I given you enough already?!"

The Withdrawn Offer

Let's say I want to buy your son's alto saxophone. You want $250, I offer $75. We haggle. You come down to $150. Hoping to close at $140 (with a case and some reeds thrown in), I offer $135. I wait. The next day you slink back to me hat in hand. "Marc, I made a terrible mistake. My boy, Jeffrey, will never forgive me if I get only $150. His friends say it's worth at least $175!" I'm outraged. "You just told me $150 was O.K.," I fume. "How can you do this to me?!"

Let's put aside the higher-authority issue (Jeffrey's friends) and analyze. By this sudden reversal, not only have you totally eroded my hope of yet a better deal, but now I'll feel lucky to buy at just $150 . . . forget the case and the reeds! What can I do? I can hold you to the $150. I can fight back, reducing my last offer and demanding that Jeffrey throw in a few free lessons. I can call you on it. Or I can use *the* classic countertactic: the walk away.

The Walk Away

Challenged by an odious opponent, you storm out in a huff. Surely there's no clearer way to draw the line. But the walk away is not only a countertactic but a legitimate gambit on its own.

Try it sometime. Don't worry about blowing your deal. If the other side doesn't come crawling after you, you can always walk right back. There's nothing to lose, except a little face. Of course, if someone walks away on you, either call their bluff and wait, or call them back and concede. In fact, actually walking away may not be necessary. A "final" offer may have the same effect.

My Last Offer

To make the most of a last, final, or best offer, choose your words very, very carefully. Not only will the phrase "take it or leave it" miff everyone but it leaves you no graceful out if someone calls your bluff. Instead, hedge. Hedge on what you're final about, hedge on when you're final, even hedge on how final you are. Deliver your "last" offer with a light touch. "This is the best I can do under the circumstances." "Why don't you think it over for a week?" "If I don't hear from you by the first, I'll have to start looking for someone else." Or, if you must, be tough, but be ready for hardball.

On the flip side, if you're the one handed a "final" offer, be sensitive to the psychology of brinkmanship. Too embarrassed to back down, a clumsy opponent may paint himself into a corner. So be diplomatic. Sidestep this tactic. How? Ignore it and keep negotiating. Or test it indirectly—for example, by suddenly becoming "unavailable" shortly before the deadline. Either way helps your opponent save face and keeps your deal on track.

Dirty Data

Is the other side feeding you bad information? Off-the-record asides, self-serving rumors, stooge intermediaries, "leaked" confidential memos, and financials with deliberate errors are all designed to use your own cleverness against you. Often dirty data is delivered through a shill. You know the caricatures: the roper who draws onlookers into a shell game, the plant who bids up auction prices. In real life, it's much sneakier. Six of the buyer's buddies make lowball offers on your home to wear you down. That hot new prospect with the golden résumé hints at all her other offers. You rush to make that key presentation only to find three of your competitors milling around the reception area. Here skepticism is your shield. Hang tough. Ignore the ruse, call them on it, or even reverse it, by letting the "competition" play itself out.

Trust Me

"Oh, we don't have to bother with that big old, complicated, formal written agreement. Trust me." This is a red flag. If your opponent suggests this, make doubly sure to get everything in writing. Read the next chapter. You'll see what I mean. By the way, whenever you hear the words "trust me," don't.

Fait Accompli

It's easier to ask forgiveness than to get permission. The fait accompli is a surprise move, done so that opposition or objection is difficult or, better yet, pointless. Do what you want, smooth everything over later. Your lawyer runs up three times his estimate, then invoices you for all of it, to see if you'll flinch. A director goes way over budget, knowing the studio must pay to finish the film, or take a bath. You get the idea.

By definition, the fait accompli is hard to anticipate. Thus, even the best due diligence, savviest street smarts, and tightest contracts may not fully protect you. These are true hardball tactics, like Hitler annexing Austria or Hussein storming Kuwait. They'll make you want to yell, sue, or hit the other side where it hurts. But cool off before you do. You don't want things to career out of control.

Getting Someone a Little Pregnant

With dinner guests set to arrive in less than an hour your plumber demands triple time, *after* he's knee-deep in goop. A general contractor hooks you with an irresistible lowball bid, knowing full well that they'll tag you for endless increases once they break ground. That sleazy literary agent overexposes your first novel to every major and minor publisher while "considering" whether to represent you.

You see the pattern. Before a deal is nailed down, one party commits the other, making it difficult, or impossible, for them to go elsewhere. It's a low tactic, hinging on a shrewd sense of timing and leverage. It's the fait accompli, but at the courtship stage. Be thankful it's also a risky tactic. A miscalculation may easily blow a deal or provoke a lawsuit. Luckily, protection is simple. Before the other side starts acting like you've got a deal, stop everything and make sure you do (and see Fig. 6.4 on page 169).

Negotiating in Bad Faith

There are times when the last thing on your opponent's mind is a deal. Beware of the hidden agenda. The other side may be fishing for proprietary information, keeping you off the market, preparing for a lawsuit, or chatting you up with some other devious design. Here negotiation in and of itself becomes a dirty trick. It doesn't happen that often, but, as usual, a skeptical nature, tight lips, and thorough due diligence are your best defenses. Remember the words of William Burroughs: "A paranoid is a man with all the facts." And take a look at figure 5.3.

THE 4 UNIVERSAL DIRTY-TRICK COUNTERTACTICS
1. Keep your cool.
2. Call them on it.
3. Walk away.
4. Strike back.

Fig. 5.3

PUTTING TIME ON YOUR SIDE

There are but ten minutes in the life of
a pear when it is perfect to eat.

—Ralph Waldo Emerson

In negotiation, power often shifts with time. For example, insurance reps know they'll have an easier time settling claims around Christmas because people need the money. Shrewd job hunters don't talk salary until the new boss says they've got to have you. Real estate players know that December 31 may spell tax disaster for one side or the other.

Time and the Shifting Sands of Leverage

Superior deal makers constantly reassess the balance of power. They anticipate when they'll have the most leverage and when they'll have the least. They always watch for the unexpected event that shifts the balance of power, such as the entry of a competitor, the approach of a deadline, or a tough break for their adversary. That's how they put time on their side. If you're in the middle of a negotiation, take a moment to review figure 5.1. Do you have more or less power than you did before?

Keep Your Fingers on the Pulse

By listening to the rhythm of the other side's responses, by phone, by fax, by mail, or by meeting, you gauge their enthusiasm, their need, and their greed. If your opponent picks up the pace, it usually means they're eager. If their responsiveness drops, their interest level probably has too.

Don't worry about looking desperate just because you keep your negotiations up-tempo. Rather, timely responses build momentum, increase focus, and enhance cooperation. And with all the details, egos, positions, interests, and technical difficulties in any halfway complicated deal, what a relief that can be!

Some strategists recommend keeping the other side off guard through change-of-pace tactics. Perhaps an occasional well-executed drop in enthusiasm may make the other side try harder. More likely, this ruse brands those who use it as manipulative, clumsy, or indecisive.

Deadlines

It's no accident that negotiations accelerate at the eleventh hour. When time is plentiful, everyone holds out for the best deal. When time is scarce, key concessions come smoothly and gracefully. Having a deadline is like having an efficiency expert seated at the bargaining table.

Discover that your opponent has real time constraints and you gain an important strategic advantage. Torque up that leverage by dragging your feet a little . . . in a nice way. A little delay, artfully disguised as mild inefficiency, droll distraction, or coincidental unavailability, goes a long way. For instance, any Hollywood agent knows to drive a much harder bargain when a studio is just days away from principal photography. Conversely, if your opponents learn you have a deadline, expect them to use it against you as well. Close your deal efficiently, without tipping your hand.

The phony deadline is a classic negotiating gambit used to force the other side into a quick close. If you suspect that a drop-dead date is bogus, test it: Press the other side for a detailed, plausible explanation, but be skeptical of what you hear. Ask for an extension to see if their reaction fits that explanation. If you can, contact an expert or an insider to verify the deadline. Or, if you feel gutsy, call their bluff. If the other side is pressuring you, often it's because they know if they really let you think things over, you'll think again.

Know When to Stop

Finally, every negotiation must come to an end. No deal is perfect, no discussion foresees every what-if, and there will always be one more point to win. Reconsider the big picture. If the expense, effort, time, lost opportunity, or increased stress outweigh the benefit of any further concessions, call it a deal and shake on it. On the flip side, once you've gone round and round on all the major issues (and most of the minor ones) and the deal still doesn't meet your bottom line, walk away. One of my clients used to say, "A good deal is like a bus—there'll be another one along in fifteen minutes."

The Close

If you want to learn something about closing a deal, hang out with salespeople. For if there's one thing a good salesperson knows how to do, it's close a deal. They live for it. Remember David Mamet's play *Glengarry Glen Ross*? "Always be closing." There are dozens and dozens of closes. Figure 5.4 lists a few.

Of course, the closes in figure 5.4 are a little glib. After all, they're geared for the simple one-shot sale. But remember, it's human nature to balk at commitment. Chalk it up to fear of the unknown. Maybe we're missing something. Maybe we'll live to regret it. Maybe, maybe, maybe, maybe, maybe. The genius of these closes is in how they elicit the real reason for the hesitation. Until you know the real objection, it will be difficult or impossible to shake on it. So study them. They'll come in handy. Here are three others that may be more suitable to the deal maker:

- *The JUST SUPPOSE close:* Once you're down to that very last objection, try something like: "Just suppose I can make this one last concession . . . will we have a deal?" It's merely another use of the condition. *If* you take care of their last concern, *then* they agree to close.
- *The T-ACCOUNT or BEN FRANKLIN close:* Supposedly, Ben Franklin used to make decisions like this. Let's say the other side has run out of objections but is still waffling. Divide a piece of paper into two columns, kind of like a T-account. On one side list the pros of the deal.

SOME STANDARD SALES CLOSES

the *alternative* close:	Would you like it in harvest gold or tropical pink?
the *assumption* close:	Should we deliver it today or tomorrow?
the *invitational* close:	Why don't you just give it a try?
the *hot button* close:	Find out the main reason the other side wants the deal, then keep hammering it home.
the *summary* or *laundry list* close:	Find out all the reasons the other side wants the deal, then list them back.
the *let me take your order* close:	Just fill in the order form as you go along, saving the name and address for last.
the *now or never* close:	This offer's good today only. Either they close or you walk away.
the *once upon a time* close:	Tell the other side a story about someone else who closed a similar deal with you with happy results.
the *let me check* close:	This is the higher authority revisited with a dose of reverse psychology. You work everything out, then tell the other side you have to check with someone else before you close.
the *put yourself in my shoes* close:	Ask them to change places with you so they can tell you the real reason they're hesitating. Once they do, you have the information you need to convince them.
the *step-by-step* close:	This is a carefully prepared series of questions, all requiring a yes answer. It builds momentum, making it easier to ask for and get that final yes.

Fig. 5.4

Help your opponent write these down. Then hand them the paper and let them fill in the second column with the cons . . . all by themselves. The combination of your help with one side and their having to go it alone on the other will probably cinch the deal.

• *The SILENT or SUDDEN DEATH close:* When you know there's nothing left to talk about, just give them the pen, hand them the contract, shut up, and wait. There's nothing like the silent treatment.

WHAT GOES AROUND . . .

In the long run, there is no long run.

—Anonymous

We've all done deals with those who live by this motto. It's cynical, mean-spirited, and, ultimately, shortsighted. This philosophy works best, if at all, in true one-shot deals, after which the two sides will never ever meet again. But outside the flea market, who does business this way? Even in the most anonymous exchange, such as selling your old car for cash through an ad, you never know when you'll need something (leniency, information, a favor) from the buyer you just fleeced. That's why I never squeeze the last drop of juice out of any deal, even when I know I can. It's no fun getting reacquainted with the person you beat up last month. You're looking for leeway; they're looking for a payback. For myself, personally, it goes even deeper than that.

In the 1920s and '30s my grandfather was a very successful merchant in a small Polish town. When times were hard, many of the peasants who frequented his general store ran up substantial debts. Grandpa never sued on these debts and often continued to extend credit or bartered with these customers. He didn't have to do it. In many cases, I'm sure it made no business sense to do it. In the early 1940s the Germans occupied that part of Poland. My grandfather was Jewish, and these customers remembered his kindness. At great risk to themselves, they hid, fed, and ultimately saved my grandfather and his family from certain extermination.

Maybe I'm being a bit too dramatic. But that's why I believe in the law of business karma. What goes around, comes around. Most deals create ongoing relationships. Beat up on people today and they'll sabotage you in a thousand little ways tomorrow. Put another way, the more one-sided the deal is for you, the more likely the other side will try to squirm out. Conversely, if you treat them decently, you'd be surprised at how cooperative, even giving, they can be.

Have Some Class

When you do cut the sharpest deal of your life, don't rub the other side's nose in it or brag so loudly that it gets back to them. Be a good sport. First-class negotiators know how to get what they want and still leave the other side feeling like a winner. They're always finding ways to help their opponents save face. After you shake on it, you still want your opponent to feel that you're caring, decent, and honorable . . . the kind of person they'd like to do business with again.

HAVING FUN

> I wanted a new TV. My wife wanted a new car. So we compromised. We got the TV, but we keep it in the garage.
>
> —Anonymous

Yes, negotiating is important, negotiating is serious, but unless you're talking down a terrorist with hostages, it's not a matter of life and death.

Cultivate your sense of humor. When things get tense, don't wait for everybody to start screaming or hissing through their teeth. Crack a joke. Medical experts agree that laughter provides wonderful physiological benefits. Business experts will tell you that laughter dissolves the tension between people, brings issues into perspective, lubricates the flow of ideas, and establishes rapport. How can communication break down when the other side is howling at the story you just put over? In one study, researchers Karen O'Quin and Joel Aronoff found that buyers who smiled and threw in their pet frog as part of their final offers were able to negotiate better deals. Anyway, from time to time we all lose our cool. Laughter will help you think more clearly.

I once worked with an Academy Award–winning producer who was the scion of a prominent and wealthy family. Somehow, someone had hired a consultant for one of his pictures who was not only glib, sleazy, and double-dealing but who, with impunity, was running the picture way over budget. To avoid an ugly lawsuit we needed to settle him out. I was so overwrought with this person that I was indignant to the point of outrage. Needless to say, I was no longer effective. My client put things into perspective. "Dino-man," he said, "just offer him a hundred bucks . . . *mostly cash!*" I burst out laughing.

Later I settled everything, quickly and effectively. So remember these words from Ken Kesey's *One Flew over the Cuckoo's Nest*: "When you lose your sense of humor, you lose your footing."

6

STEP 6:

WRITE IT DOWN

Nothing makes fine print more legible
than an accident.

—*The Wall Street Journal*

At last . . . the final step. The time has come to seal the deal, to look that person across the table in the eye, stick out your hand, and say, "Let's shake on it."

There's just one more thing. You need to memorialize your understanding, not just with drinks and dinner or gleeful phone calls and splashy press releases, but by a formal agreement. And so welcome to the wonderful world of written contracts, to that dreary dimension of deeds, documents, and dotted lines.

To me, this sixth and last step is both a climax and a letdown. It's the act of conception and your kid's tuition bill rolled into one. Because after all is said and done, after all the drama of deliberating, negotiating, and closing the deal, what remains is the contract, the formal document that you and the world will study as the blueprint of your deal.

SIX REASONS TO ALWAYS GET IT IN WRITING

To break an oral agreement which is not
legally binding is morally wrong.

—Talmud, Baba Metzia

Men keep their agreements when it is an
advantage to both parties not to break them.

—Solon

Oral agreements may be just as binding as written ones, but they're not nearly as easy to prove. Of course, there are exceptions. After losing a $9 million lawsuit for breach of oral contract Kim Basinger must have winced at Samuel Goldwyn's famous: "A verbal agreement isn't worth the paper it's printed on." Nevertheless, the written word carries much more weight. Even if you don't count lawsuits, there are still many great reasons to write things down.

1. To Remind Each Party of What Was Agreed

As we all know, memories are short and often convenient. And it's not just a matter of creating evidence for your day in court. One of the tackier things I did as a fledgling attorney was to send my new boss a letter confirming the details of my job offer. This was not politically astute, especially at the beginning of a new, and presumably beautiful, relationship. As it turned out, later, we did disagree on my salary review, which was supposed to take place at six months (as I stated), rather than a full year (as he assumed). Showing him the letter convinced him. If he didn't see it my way, could I have vindicated myself in court? Absolutely. Would I have? Not unless I wanted every future employer to see me as petty and litigious.

But if individual memories are short, corporate memories are ephemeral. The groundbreaking concessions you hammered out with one executive may mean nothing to their replacement . . . unless you can prove it with paper. A written agreement is evidence not only for the parties who originally struck the deal but for those who later have to live with it.

Ironically, when we deal with friends, it's even more important to write it down. Sure, some pals work on a handshake and solve problems fairly at the time. But who hasn't been shocked by how different friends are when it comes to business? With all the emotions, history, and unspoken assumptions underlying friendship, bruised feelings and falling outs are just waiting to happen.

MONEY: THE DETAILS OF PAYMENT

BASIC QUESTIONS

What?   all of it?
part of it?
    half now, half later?
    quarters, thirds, or some other division?
installments?
    equal or unequal?
    how many?
    at what interval?
    for how long?
tax or other withholdings?
some combination of all of the above?

When?   in advance?
when the contract's signed?
after goods are received, or services rendered?
after a set period of time?
after a specific condition is satisfied?
some combination of all of the above?

How?   cash?
check?
credit card?
other? (notes, letters of credit)
some combination of all of the above?

Who?   an individual?
more than one individual?
an entity, such as a partnership or corporation?
some combination of all of the above?

Where?   address?
    by mail?
    by hand?
    in person?
    by courier service?
    by wire transfer?
    some combination of all of the above?

Fig. 6.1 *(continued on following page)*

Fig. 6.1 *(continued)*

RELATED QUESTIONS

what if one party goes bankrupt?

what if one party can't pay because of an act of
God? because of an act of a third party?
because of their own act?

what if a party simply refuses to pay?

what if a party pays late?

if interest is payable, how is it calculated?

if foreign currency is involved, how is the exchange rate
calculated?

what events, if any, would excuse payment?

can the party being paid request that payment be
made to a third party instead?

can the paying party offset payment by the amount(s)
owed to it by the party being paid?

if payment is based on profits, how will profit be calculated, and verified?

---

2. It Will Make You a Sharper, More Thorough Deal Maker

Putting pen to paper will make you think. It'll force you to be specific. Sure, by this time in a deal you know the broad strokes—for example, the how much. But even something as basic as paying money involves numerous details, many of them essential. Just glance at figure 6.1.

Writing also invites us to fill in the landscape. After all, a written agreement is the instruction manual for the relationship. Let's say someone gets sick, or the inspection turns up something, or a union member has a grievance . . . what do we do? It alerts us to holes and risks we missed before. In a way, it's a secondary line of quality control for what we either didn't spot or didn't have time for earlier.

3. In Ongoing Relationships, Written Contracts Position Us for the Inevitable: The Next Round of Negotiations

Lew Wasserman, the CEO of MCA, Inc., and one of the great entertainment deal makers, has one of the savviest reasons for signing agreements: to establish a starting point for settlement discussions. Truly, a written contract is often just a resting point in the giant ongoing negotiation that characterizes long-term relationships. Collective-bargaining agreements are perfect examples. Players in the oil industry are inextricably fused together; their deals ebb and flow with the forces of economics and politics, one agreement positioning the participants for the next.

4. So We Have a Stronger Lawsuit If the Other Side Breaches

A written agreement is strong evidence, and its very existence encourages the parties to honor it. The specter of litigation is always present. As we'll see in Chapter 9, the time, cost, and aggravation of suing make it a true last resort. But if worse comes to worst, a strong contract can be crucial not only to winning a lawsuit but to preventing one in the first place.

5. Because Various Laws Require Written Contracts

Courts simply will not enforce certain agreements unless they're in writing. In 1676 the English passed "An Act for Prevention of Frauds and Perjuries." More commonly known as the the Statute of Frauds, it's still alive and well in our law. Generally, it requires that certain types of contracts be in writing; see figure 6.2. But that's only part of the story. As you can also see from figure 6.2, laws unrelated to the Statute of Frauds might also require a signed writing.

Outside the courtroom, there are other good legal reasons to get it in writing. Good documentation is critical if you're audited. If a parent lends a child money, a promissory note can be the key to dividing the estate fairly; otherwise, how do you separate a gift from a loan? By the way, the next time you're representing a basketball star, remember that the NBA collective-bargaining agreement also requires that his contract be a written one.

THE STATUTE OF FRAUDS: DEALS A COURT WON'T ENFORCE UNLESS THEY ARE IN WRITING

Statute of Frauds—Basic Categories
1. a promise to pay someone else's debt
2. contracts for the sale of land (or any interest in land)
3. contracts for the sale of goods over $500
4. contracts that cannot be performed within one year
5. contracts in consideration of marriage (but not a mutual promise to marry)
6. contracts that cannot be performed during the lifetime of the promisor

Other State Laws Requiring Written Agreements
1. contracts giving an agent the right to enter into a contract that is within the Statute of Frauds
2. contracts for the sale of securities
3. contracts involving a security interest in personal property, crops, or fixtures
4. contracts to pay debts after the Statute of Limitations has run out
5. contracts to pay debts discharged in bankruptcy
6. contracts involving certain consumer transactions, such as vehicle repair, warranties, and loans
7. certain grants of rights under copyright law

WARNING! This is just a thumbnail guide. Litigants have been arguing over, and judges have been applying, this statute for over three hundred years. Actual laws vary from state to state and are crusty with exceptions, definitions, interpretations, and complications . . . just ask anyone studying for the bar.

Fig. 6.2

6. As Ritual, to Cement Our Commitments

Finally, we draft and sign contracts for ceremonial value. In our ritual-impoverished society, it's one of the few rites left us. It's a symbolic and defining act, just another way of saying, "Let's shake on it."

TAKING CHARGE OF THE PAPERS

"When *I* use a word," Humpty Dumpty said, in rather a
scornful tone, "it means just what I choose it to
mean—neither more nor less."

"The question is," said Alice, "whether you *can* make
words mean so many different things."

"The question is," said Humpty Dumpty, "which is to
be master—that's all."

—Lewis Carroll, *Through the Looking-Glass*

One of the best things you can do when you close a deal is to be the
one preparing the contracts. True, this isn't always possible. Sometimes custom dictates otherwise; other times the stronger party, such
as a bank, will insist on using its own forms. And when you're on
unfamiliar ground, you may, for tactical reasons and to mask your
inexperience, let the other side go first. But generally, your carefully
chosen wording gives you the upper hand. Among other things, it lets
you pinpoint the other side's obligations with irritating precision
while leaving elbow room on yours. As we saw in Step 4, choice
clauses can also give you an edge at trial. That's why real estate
lawyers use one batch of forms when they represent the landlord and
another when they represent the tenant.

Taking charge of the paperwork also lets you control the negotiation in a subtle way. Your choice as to the size, complexity, and number of documents can either facilitate or frustrate. What you put in
that first draft can flush out hidden problems. For instance, as we saw
in Step 4, if you're not sure the other side has the right to do something, ask them to warrant and represent that they can in writing. The
draft documents you circulate can provide a graceful approach to a
touchy issue, a strategy to make up or gain ground, or a remedy for
missteps.

Consider Using Shorter Contracts

It may cost more to have your lawyer draw up a contract, rather than
to just respond to one, but ultimately it can save you time and money.
To explain this, I'll vent about one of my pet peeves. Kafka defined
lawyers as the only persons who write a ten-thousand-word document

and call it a brief. Deal makers hate long contracts, and, in my opinion, most contracts are way too long.

Many lawyers won't agree. Perhaps, in very sophisticated business transactions, they've got a point. When matters are complex and big dollars are involved, or if you question the other side's integrity, then details and increased legal protection are very important. But more often, lawyers play on the legal fears of their clients, selling them overly comprehensive documents like garrulous insurance agents hawking superfluous coverages. Long documents gum things up. Legalese makes them unreadable. Their needless restatement of well-settled principles of law brews discord. Ironically, despite their obsessive preoccupation with remote contingencies, thick documents are often not only ineffective in anticipating actual courtroom battles but inapplicable to reality as it actually unfolds. Long forms are the refuge of paranoid practitioners who don't trust themselves or their clients, and shifty attorneys who boost their billables by manufacturing crises.

Maybe you think I'm overstating my case. Regardless, this is a good place to control your lawyer. If your side is preparing papers, carefully monitor what you send out. Every paragraph is another paragraph that has to be drafted, reviewed, commented on, discussed, negotiated, revised, approved . . . and billed for! Deals should not stall out over boilerplate. An effective draftsperson can make it shorter, easier, and cheaper to close your deal.

How to Prepare Your Own Contracts

How about those times when it doesn't make sense to hire an attorney to prepare your contracts? You should still get something in writing. Try your local stationery store. You'll be surprised at how many "tear off the pad and fill in the blank" legal forms are available; for pennies, they may sell you one that does the trick. You may also find the perfect book or magazine article, with the contract or guidelines you need, at the public library or a bookstore. Or try the Internet. One word of warning: Reread any form carefully before you use it. You don't want the preprinted provisions to conflict with or contradict the specifics of your deal.

Finally, if all else fails, take your best shot and do it yourself. Here's a short checklist of items you should include in contracts you prepare:

1. the names and addresses of the parties;
2. the date the agreement is supposed to take effect;
3. a description of what the other side's supposed to do (including when, where, and for how long);
4. a description of what you're supposed to do (including when, where, and for how long);
5. a description of what each side is not responsible for;
6. an integration clause (see page 101);
7. a place for each party to sign; and
8. the date the parties signed.

Look at the form in figure 6.3. As you can see, you can set it up as a letter. Be as specific as you can when you're describing things and naming people, companies, and dates. You may think it takes great sophistication to describe a deal accurately. Certainly a lawyer should do a better job than a layperson. But if you apply Rudyard Kipling's six honest serving men from Step 1 (What, Why, When, How, Where, and Who), you shouldn't go too far astray. Also consider attaching what you describe in your contract as exhibits—for example, pictures, sample materials, and drawings—to show what was intended. If possible, label these exhibits to refer back to the main contract and have everyone initial or sign those exhibits. Also, if you later handwrite changes to an agreement that's typed, make sure each party initials each change, as well.

Of course, Figure 6.3 is no substitute for your own attorney and is not intended as legal advice. But whether your homemade contract is a model of elegant simplicity or one with gaping holes, it'll almost always serve you better than a mere handshake.

Proofread

Don't forget to proofread your paperwork. You'd be shocked at the amount of litigation arising out of misspellings, incorrect descriptions, improper corporate names, and the like. If you make a truly outrageous mistake, don't worry . . . you'll probably be able to fix it (with some embarrassment), but if your typo is one the other side would be reasonable in relying on as an accurate statement of the deal, you may be stuck with your mistake. If you only have two seconds to proof, at least make sure the line that starts "You shall pay . . ." has the right amount.

A MODEL FOR HOMEMADE LETTER AGREEMENTS

[Your Name]
[Your Address]
[Your Phone Number] [optional]

as of: [the date the agreement
is supposed to be effective]

[The Other Side's Name]
[The Other Side's Address]

Re: [A basic statement of what this deal is about]

Dear _____:

The following shall constitute our agreement as follows:

1. Numbered paragraphs describing how, what, when, where, and for how long you have to do what you're supposed to do.
2. Numbered paragraphs describing how, what, when, where, and for how long the other side has to do what they're supposed to do.

[If money is changing hands, remember figure 6.1.]
[If it'll help you describe things better, attach exhibits.]

3. Consider additional numbered paragraphs describing what each side does not have to do or is not responsible for.
4. This agreement contains our entire understanding and cannot be changed orally. [This should be your last paragraph.]

Very truly yours,

[Sign Your Name]
[Type Your Name]

AGREED:

_____
[a line for the other side to sign]

_____
[a line for the other side to print or type their name]

ACTUAL DATE OF SIGNING: _____

Fig. 6.3

Keep Good Files

Make it a habit to take fresh and accurate notes of events and conversations. For clarity, use different color inks to record different conversations. Hold onto all versions of paperwork. Keep originals, rather than copies, of important documents. Consider the section "Preserve Evidence" on page 211. This will not only enhance your negotiating and overall deal making but position you well in case of a lawsuit.

Some trial lawyers would disagree with this. Because the rules of discovery (see fig. 9.1 on page 215) generally give your opponent broad license to sift through your file cabinet, they feel anything you say, or write and keep, may be used against you. Still, I think more litigators would have you keep files in order—assuming you have no smoking guns, of course. This is largely due to a legal technicality: the exceptions to the *parol evidence rule* and the failure of an integration clause (see page 101) to eliminate them. It's worth explaining.

Basically, at trial, the parol evidence rule bars evidence that points to other parts of your deal that you didn't write down. Like the integration clause, it maintains the integrity of written contracts as complete expressions of a deal. Unfortunately, the exceptions almost swallow the rule. It doesn't apply to evidence that the written agreement was not complete, or *integrated*, to evidence that is needed to interpret (but not to add to or vary) unclear wording, or to evidence that *vitiates* agreement (such as evidence of fraud). Even using an elaborate or superbroad integration clause, like "Nothing that was said during our negotiations may be used for any purpose whatsoever," may not fully protect you. Thus, anything said or done before, or at the time, the deal was signed could be key. Having the better record will give you more control over the evidence introduced at trial.

Keep good files. Learn from Sam Goldwyn. When his secretary asked him if she could throw away files that had been inactive for ten years he said, "Go ahead, but make sure you keep copies."

UNDERSTANDING THE FINE PRINT

The minute you read something you don't understand,
you can be almost sure it was drawn up by a lawyer.
—Will Rogers

Coping with Legalese

The impenetrability of legalese has a long and glorious history, one that's not only amusing but instructive. During the Middle Ages, the Irish *brehons*, or jurists, actually scrambled the words and sentences of their lawbooks to make them unreadable without a secret code. Some of their manuscripts have taken fifty years to decipher. Recently, the Texas State Bar instituted annual Legaldegook Awards to honor especially horrible legal writing. Here's the winner of the 1991 Rise-of-the-Roman-Language Award: "Parens patriae cannot be ad fundandam jurisdictionem. The zoning question is res inter alios acta." That's a fancy way for a judge to say that his court doesn't have jurisdiction.

Why is legal language so opaque? For one thing, it maintains the lawyer's monopoly. Incomprehensible wording keeps the uninitiated out and gives attorneys a way to justify high fees. It's a marketing strategy that creates a consumer need based on confusion and anxiety. Legalese also comes out of the law's innate conservatism. Baby lawyers are raised with poor models; inertia and the fear of changing what already works preserve the status quo. Peer pressure is also a factor. Every clique has its own unique lingo: doctors, barbers, surfers, gangsters. Lawyers are no different. Finally, legalese is a tactic. It lets the lawyer bob and weave. With these magical mantras, the attorney can lock in the other side's obligations while giving his or her side the option to avoid its own.

The antidote to legalese is the Plain English Movement. Its proponents promote the use of precise words, simple sentences, and clear, accessible outlines and denounce convoluted grammar, archaic language, and ornate formalisms. To paraphrase legal writing expert David Mellinkoff, look at the way some contracts start:

> WITNESSETH, this Agreement (hereinafter sometimes referred to as the "Agreement") is made and entered into as of the 31st day of January, 1997, in the County of Los Angeles, State of California, by and between MARC DIENER (hereinafter sometimes referred to as the "Party of the First Part"), on the one hand, and the COGSWELL COGS CORPORATION, a corporation duly organized and validly existing in accordance with the laws of the State of East Carolina (hereinafter sometimes referred to as the "Party of the Second Part"), on the other hand.

Here's the same contract in plain English:

January 31, 1997
Los Angeles, California

MARC DIENER and the COGSWELL COGS CORPORATION agree as
follows:

I wish all contracts were this easy to read. Unfortunately, despite its
growing acceptance, the Plain English Movement has a long way to
go. But legalese is more than just annoying; it can be treacherous as
well. For example, I once knew an entrepreneur who turned his
garage-based business into a multimillion-dollar outfit. But somewhere along the way, he let a couple of crafty investors bail him out of
a perilous cash crunch. The details didn't seem important then, but
the money was. Hastily, he signed on the dotted line—not realizing he
was also ceding them control. Inevitably, friction developed. Within
months those investors fired him from the company he created,
throwing him out of his own office!

That little something in legalese the other guy wants you to sign
may look harmless, but it's not. Get an English translation. Call your
lawyer.

"Standard" Terms and Conditions

At one time or another, we've all been handed the so-called standard
form. These forms deserve a special digression. Sometimes they're fair
and useful. In international trade, for instance, they're not only a sort
of prefab compromise that speeds up negotiations but they smooth
out conflicting rules among different countries. In their depraved
form, however, they mutate into the infamous *contract of adhesion*.

A contract of adhesion is the standard form presented to the consumer on a take-it-or-leave-it basis. Filled with vintage legaldegook
and onerous one-sided boilerplate, it's the fine print in your automobile purchase agreement, those itsy-bitsy words on your baseball
tickets, or those dense paragraphs on the back of that whatever-that-
you-never-bother-reading. They often include "in terrorem" clauses
designed to scare the little guy into submission. This negotiating tactic
also works well outside the consumer context. There is a tremendous
perceived legitimacy to preprinted Standard Terms and Conditions.

They help an executive keep a straight face when he or she says: "Oh, we never change that," or "Sorry, that's our policy," or simply, "Take it or leave it."

Can you protect yourself against these forms? Not really. You could walk away every time you're given one, but that will cripple you as a consumer. Some negotiating gurus proclaim there's no such thing as a standard form and that everything's negotiable. I disagree. The next time you feel like testing this, try tuning up the boilerplate on your airline ticket . . . and please, let me know if you make your flight. The good news, on the other hand, is that courts don't like these contracts. Often judges will rescue consumers from trick clauses slipped in by reference, buried on the reverse side, or set in subatomic type. After all, if a loophole defeats the very purpose of a contract, it would be unjust to enforce it. Yet you may have to hire a lawyer to prove your point.

How to Read a Contract

Let's say you're handed an obnoxious standard-form contract. It's not worth the time or money to have your lawyer go over it, and you know you'll end up signing it anyway. Should you still read it? Yes. Just because you can't change the terms doesn't mean you should ignore them. That time-deposit agreement may let the bank automatically redeposit your money *unless you notify them otherwise within a certain time period*. It's a pain to calendar a notice two years in advance, but if you don't learn the rules, you may be stuck.

When you must read agreements without the help of a lawyer, follow these rules:

1. *Read slowly; read every single word.* Reviewing contracts can be incredibly boring. Be prepared to spend some time. This may sound like unremarkable advice, but even experienced attorneys miss obvious traps when they get antsy.

2. *Read literally.* At their best, contracts are scientific in their precision. Approach these documents very concretely.

3. *Go back and double-check all the cross-references.* Again, read literally.

4. *Watch out for defined terms.* Insurance companies really limit their exposure by the way they define "covered loss," "insurable event," and the like. In the music business, some record companies routinely define "net sales" as 85 percent of actual sales. It may or may not be justified, but it does mean that everytime you read the phrase "net sales," you're getting 85 percent of what you think, like it or not.

5. *If you don't know what it means, ask.* Try to get an intelligent answer (in writing, if possible).

6. *Watch out for legal mumbo jumbo.* Legalese is slippery. Beware the following:

- "notwithstanding," "subject to," "provided that," "conditioned on," and sometimes "upon" and "after" (all elegant ways of saying "but," i.e., there's a catch)
- "and" and "or" (misreading these can make a big difference)
- "or otherwise" (one of the great catchalls)
- "and/or" (does this mean "and" or "or" or both, and who gets to decide this anyway?)
- "pursuant to," "in accordance with" (sneaky cross-references)
- "deemed" (a second cousin to the defined term)
- "above," "aforementioned," "aforesaid," "below," "following," "forthwith," "foregoing," "hereinafter, -above -before," "heretofore," "preceding" (they're all vague)
- any words in Latin

Finally, never forget that the printed word is mightier than the spoken one. That loan officer may assure you that you've got four years to repay, but if what you actually sign is a promissory note payable *on demand*, you could have an unexpected problem.

BUT I NEVER SIGNED IT!

> Mephistopheles: I'll bring you please a couple lines to sign.
> Faust: So, black and white you want? You've never heard
>   Good pedant, that a man may keep his word?
> —Goethe, *Faust*

There's a common misconception that a deal ain't a deal until you sign on the dotted line. This is not only wrong but dangerous. One general exception is the handshake or oral agreement. Another specific one arose during the celebrated Pennzoil-Texaco case and is a serious example every deal maker should study.

Pennzoil vs. Texaco

On December 28, 1983, Pennzoil offered to buy the Getty Oil Company. On January 2, 1984, after just six days of negotiating, a *memorandum of agreement* was prepared and signed by Pennzoil but not by Getty. On January 4, Getty issued a press release announcing the merger, subject to the execution of a definitive agreement. But, apparently, sometime between January 3 and January 5, Getty also started talking to Texaco, because on January 6 Texaco announced that it had bought Getty!

Sometimes called a *deal letter* or an *agreement in principle* (or even a *letter of intent*, which is a less binding variation), a memorandum of agreement is a tidy rest stop between mere negotiations and the signing of long formal documents. It's quick. It nails down agreed points to avoid rehashing them. It encourages people to work together. But is it a deal? Is it a deal if it leaves out an important point? Is it a deal if it states that the parties will continue negotiating until longer papers are signed? Is it a deal if only one party signs? In this case, Pennzoil sure thought it had a deal. It sued Texaco for interfering with it and won . . . $10.6 billion!

How could this have happened?! Not only had Getty not signed, but it had publicly proclaimed that the merger was conditioned on a definitive agreement. Besides, how could such sophisticated deal makers wind up in court arguing over something so basic as whether or not they even had a deal? To illuminate this, let me "offer" you a little taste of one of the unique intellectual delights of first-year law school: contracts.

Contracts 101: "Offer, Acceptance, Consideration"

Business civilizations produce contract law. You really don't find it in precommercial societies. They have other ways of enforcing obligations—for example, through ties of kinship or the power of religion. Put another way, a caveman's idea of collateral didn't involve mortgages, liens, or trust deeds. He just took hostages. Roman contract law dates back to Justinian and the sixth century A.D. and has grown ever since, paralleling the increasing complexity of the commercial world.

So, how do you define a contract? It's a lot like how you define a deal. In *Black's Law Dictionary*, the standard legal dictionary, it's "an agreement between two or more persons which creates an obligation to do or not to do a particular thing." Think of it as a mutual promise. Now, every law student knows that three things are needed to form a contract: *offer, acceptance*, and *consideration*. Simple? Hardly!

The American Law Institute, a group of American legal scholars, publishes "Restatements" that set out the generally accepted rules of a body of law, how those rules are changing, and what direction the authors feel the law should take. The Restatement of Contracts declares: "An offer is the manifestation of willingness to enter into a bargain, so made as to justify another person in understanding that his assent to that bargain is invited and will conclude it." So far, so good, but . . .

What if you make an offer, but you were just kidding? How about an advertisement—is that an offer? If you use the words "Would you pay?" is that an offer, or are you just bargaining? What if you offer someone two alternatives and they accept without making a choice? What if you mail an offer by mistake? What if you make an offer but leave out something critical? What if you want to revoke an offer, but the other person has already spent time or money on it?

Turn back to the Restatement of Contracts. "Acceptance of an offer is a manifestation of assent to the terms thereof made by the offeree in a manner invited or required by the offer." Again, this isn't simple. What if I accept, but I grumble about it? What if I accept, but add just one condition? What if I don't say anything? What if my acceptance and the other person's revocation cross in the mail?

As for consideration, one court defined it as "Some right, interest, profit or benefit accruing to one party, or some forbearance, detriment, loss, or responsibility, given, suffered, or undertaken by the other." I'll translate: There has to be something "in it" for both sides. Today, the doctrine of consideration has become so convoluted and riddled with holes that I'm not sure legal scholars, much less the state bar examiners, can really pin it down. Offer, acceptance, consideration . . . now you see why Oliver Wendell Holmes once said, "If you can eat sawdust without butter, you can be a success in the Law."

Out in the real world you're constantly forming contracts: when you buy a movie ticket, when you order in a restaurant, when you pick up that nasty little disclaimer from the parking attendant. These deals are part written, part oral, and part implied. They're standard, usually cause no problem, and can be analyzed easily using traditional notions of offer, acceptance, and consideration. But as we apply these principles to more sophisticated transactions, deal making gets treacherous.

Let's return to the "it's got to be signed on the dotted line" fallacy. Did you know, for example, that if a party intends something as a signature, they can sign anywhere on the contract, by pen, pencil, lithograph, rubber stamp, initial, fingerprint, or any other kind of mark? If a contract boldly states that it must be signed in duplicate, it's still valid even if only one copy is signed. Not everyone need sign the same piece of paper if they sign counterparts. Actually, it doesn't even have to be a piece of paper anymore, since some courts recognize computer-generated electronic contracts as binding. In fact, several writings, such as an exchange of letters or faxes, can be read together to form a contract. To complicate things, consider the legal doctrine of *promissory estoppel*. Basically, it says that if you make someone a reasonable promise and they rely on it to their detriment, you will be held to that promise; in other words, you've got a deal—like it or not.

The Deal Maker . . . Unbound

So imagine yourself a fly on the wall at Getty, Pennzoil, or Texaco sometime between December 28, 1983, and January 6, 1984. In the heat of negotiations, in the center of that windstorm of phone calls, faxes, letters, and meetings, with dozens of different legal principles and their variations to consider, can you see how easy it is to lose track of when you've really "shaken on it"? To me this is one of the great ironies of deal making. The shrewdest businesspeople, the sharpest lawyers, the cleverest financial people, the most competent of the competent can *and do* miss the most fundamental point of all: whether or not they have a deal!

This is a sobering lesson for every deal maker. Who knows? Maybe Texaco took a calculated risk. Just keep in mind that you never know when a judge or jury will say you've crossed the threshold from discussion to commitment. The sad reality is this: *There is no nifty rule of thumb or surefire litmus test to know when you have a deal!* On one end of the spectrum, a detailed unconditional, formal legal document signed by both parties will almost always mean there's a deal. Why "almost always"? Because even a seemingly airtight written contract may be vulnerable to a clever legal attack. Other times, it's shades of gray. Courts will look at everything: express statements; whether correspondence is in the future tense; what's been agreed to; whether the deal is so complex or the parties so sophisticated that one would expect them to wait until formal papers are signed; whether they're acting like they have a deal; whether they've issued press releases or thrown parties; and so on.

Here we have one of the trickiest issues a deal maker can finesse. It would be easy for me to say that if you don't want to be bound until the ink's dry, make sure you say so, loud and clear, but that could chill your negotiations. On the other hand, you don't want to bind or not bind yourself by mistake. Take heed of Texaco. If it happened to them, it could happen to you.

LAWYER'S TRICKS

> They do tricks even I can't figure out.
> —Harry Houdini on lawyers

Talking to a lawyer can be slippery. Between all the *perhaps*es, *likely*s, *in my opinion*s, and *as the case may be*s, you never get a straight answer. Yet it's with the written word that our aggressive advocates really earn their hourly rate. We've already hinted at a few tactics: the deal letter and irritating preprinted standard terms and conditions. Below are a few other tricks of the trade. Figure 6.5 contains a neat summary.

Hiding the Ball

Imagine an ad for "the device that kills bugs every time." Sound great? You mail in your check, including postage and handling, only to receive two blocks of wood with the following instructions: "Place bug between blocks and press firmly." Thank the advertising world for this textbook example of the technique I call *hiding the ball*. It is a cherished and universal tactic among all shrewd miscommunicators. In deal making, let's define it as malicious obedience to the literal meaning of words subtly chosen by one side because the other is likely to misinterpret them. It's a verbal cloaking device. It originates with the merchant's fear of commitment and the lawyer's compulsion to condition and qualify every utterance.

My favorite story involves an ex-lawyer turned biographer who didn't want to reveal that his uncle went to the chair for murder. He wrote, "Ebenezer occupied a chair of applied electronics at one of our leading governmental institutions. He was attached to his position by the strongest ties. His death came as a true shock."

Now, these examples are cute. But be advised that a skilled word-smith can pick your pocket with a well-turned phrase. The ball is hidden in meticulously worded notice paragraphs full of technical snares, in surgical cross-references to misleading sub-subparagraphs, and in ordinary words given extraordinary meanings like the notorious net profit definition in movie contracts (which Eddie Murphy once called "monkey points," presumably because they're rarely worth anything). When you owe me money, I want the "how much" and "when" specified with the phrase "You shall pay me . . ." When I owe you money I might avoid "I shall pay you" and instead word it this way: "You shall be entitled to . . ." You ask, "What's the difference?" Well, if I've been cheated and you come calling for your money, I will look you straight in the eye and tell you: "No one is *entitled* to that money more than you are, but the contract doesn't say that I'm the one who's supposed to pay!" If you think this too facile to work, imagine a deal with more than two parties. I may put you off indefinitely by claiming that some third party is the real culprit. Is my phrasing aboveboard? Obviously not. But if you think you'll need to protect yourself, it's very, very practical.

On the other hand, if you're on defense, worry. It's always easier to be the one seeding the minefield than the one crawling through it. Where you find ambiguity or questionable wording that you suspect may be used against you, do your best to negotiate changes to the phrasing of the contract that are crystal clear.

The Reliance Letter

In the ideal world of deals, all agreements would be written down and signed. However, deals are often struck without time to hash out a contract, or knowing full well that the other side won't commit in writing. In fact, sending out an agreement that never gets signed can look worse for you than never sending one out at all. When this is so, a *reliance letter* is a good second choice.

Basically, a reliance letter confirms an oral agreement and adds a legal hook at the end: "If the terms contained in this letter are not a completely accurate description of our agreement, please notify me in writing immediately as I will rely on these terms in moving forward with our agreement." The reliance letter is a first cousin to promissory estoppel (described earlier). Essentially, it warns the other side that you're about to spend time and money or lose other opportunities because of your deal, putting the onus on them to write you immediately if you shouldn't. The longer they wait to respond, the more you *relied* and the more binding the deal becomes. When appropriate, you can even give them a deadline. It also helps to copy a bunch of people on your letter. Keep in mind that the sample language I've supplied will hit the other side in the teeth. If you want to be a little smoother, try: "Please let me know if I haven't described our deal accurately." When used artfully, a reliance letter floats like a butterfly and stings like a bee. Luckily, the countertactic is simple. If you receive a letter that's inaccurate, just set the record straight by writing back, promptly.

The Letter of Intent

The *letter of intent* is simply a less binding, or even nonbinding, version of the deal letter or memorandum of agreement, a statement of one party's intention to do a deal on certain terms, subject to certain conditions. See the previous section ("But I Never Signed It!") and especially figure 6.4. All the same rules apply. The letter of intent is really more of a gesture designed to keep things moving than a real piece of paper. But as always, it's all in the wording. A crafty letter of intent may either protect one from a premature commitment or suck the unwary into one. Never sign one that isn't crystal clear about what is and isn't intended to be binding.

Accord and Satisfaction

Finally, here's one more classic: Say you're arguing with someone who you think owes you $1,000 for something. Their lawyer sends you a check for $500 with the words "Paid in full" written on it. You don't know when, or if, you'll ever see the other $500, so you figure you'll cash this check and try for the rest later. Don't! In most states, under the doctrine of *accord and satisfaction*, you've just settled your claim for fifty cents on the dollar. This rule developed as a fast way for merchants to settle disputed claims. Remember, accepting money or cashing a check is always a legally significant act. Check with your friendly neighborhood attorney first.

HOW TO AVOID GETTING
ROPED INTO A DEAL PREMATURELY

Do notify the other side in writing that you will not be bound until you've signed on the dotted line.

Do repeat the above step in every piece of written correspondence.

Do place a legend on every legal document you circulate that reads
> DRAFT—FOR DISCUSSION PURPOSES ONLY—NOT INTENDED
> TO BE A LEGALLY BINDING DOCUMENT.

Do insert contingencies, conditions, approvals, and the like into your negotiations.

Do refer to any "proposed" agreement using the future tense and the conditional mood. For example, "the agreement we might enter into if we can negotiate a fair price."

Do not make any statement inconsistent with the above.

Do not agree to any important point without specifically conditioning it on your agreement to every other point, whether major or minor.

Do not throw parties, make announcements, or take any public action that would make others think you've struck a deal.

Do not begin to perform your side of the bargain.

Do not let the other side perform their side; let them know in writing that they do so at their own risk.

Fig. 6.4

THE GOOD, THE BAD, AND THE UGLY

CHICO: You know, Miss Dimp, my brudder got trown in jail because he had sinus trouble.

MISS DIMPLE: Thrown in jail for "sinus trouble"?

CHICO: Yeah. He sinus name to a bad check.

> —from *"Flywheel, Shyster and Flywheel":*
> *The Marx Brothers' Lost Radio Show*

COMMON LAWYER'S TRICKS

Name	What It Is	How or Why It's Used	Recognizing It	Handling or Avoiding It
Legalese	The language of the law	To impress and confuse the layperson	Formal, wordy, redundant, and/or archaic language	Get your lawyer to translate.
"Standard" Terms and Conditions	Legal "boilerplate" often filled with waivers, releases, and exculpatory clauses	To standardize transactions and/or get a leg up on the other side	Preprinted forms with unreadable type or long, formal documents full of legal mumbo jumbo	If you have leverage, negotiate changes.
Letter of Intent	A short letter indicating a party's interest in doing a deal along certain lines	To generate interest in a negotiation without binding anyone	Letter is pleasant but noncommittal.	If you want a real commitment, get another letter that spells it out.
"Deal Letter" or "Agreement in Principle"	Short-form agreement focusing on essential deal terms	To nail down basic points in complex deals so parties can move forward while resolving "minor" issues	Short agreements (often in letter form) that deal with "bare bones" terms; may refer to a long-form agreement to be signed later	See figure 6.4 and "But I Never Signed It!" on pages 162–66.

Reliance Letter	A letter that confirms an agreement by the recipient's silence	To bind someone to an agreement without their signature	Letter will request that you respond to the sender if the deal has been misstated	Always respond promptly (in writing) to inaccurate correspondence.
"Hide the Ball" Drafting	Slick wording that seems to mean one thing but actually means another	• To trick one side into thinking they've gotten something they haven't • To allow the drafting party to sidestep its obligations	The better the draftperson, the tougher it is	• See "How to Read a Contract" on pages 161–62. • Negotiate specific changes to the wording of the document.
Accord and Satisfaction	A new agreement reached to settle an old claim	At its most efficient, one party simply sends a "fair" amount to the aggrieved party, hoping they'll accept it.	Sudden receipt of partial payments of disputed amounts, often by checks or with correspondence mentioning "settlement" or "payment in full"	Don't accept partial payments of disputed amounts; call your lawyer. (*Note*: Laws vary from state to state.)

Fig. 6.5

The techniques I just described range from shrewd to sneaky. Personally, I'd use the latter for defense only. But now we move from the merely questionable to the downright fishy, from the kinda dicey to the outright criminal.

Fraudulent Documents

Forged signatures, replaced pages, retyped wording, and the like are a nasty reality for the deal maker. (I tried but couldn't find any cases that involved reappearing invisible ink.) The photocopier was the best thing to happen to the document doctor since the invention of tracing paper. And, of course, now there are computers with desk-top publishing capability. Can you safeguard against fraudulent documents? Well, "had we but world enough and time," you'd have a document examiner go over every line. But that's like protecting against food poisoning by bringing your personal taster and lab technician to every restaurant. Here are some practical precautions:

   1. *Use your own eyes; inspect.* On July 21, 1992, colorful Italian financier Giancarlo Parretti, who at one time controlled MGM, was indicted for offering altered corporate documents into evidence. The paper in question was a fax that had phony datelines pasted on it from another fax. Sometimes forgers are sloppy. If even *you* can see the outline where a valid signature was cut out and photocopied over a damaging document . . .
   2. *Keep* originals *of important papers.* Even an amateur can produce a respectable counterfeit with a copier.
   3. *Keep copies of everything . . . especially of what you send out.* Make sure it all comes back without hidden alterations.
   4. *Before you send documents out for signature, initial each page.* It's simple to slip phony pages into long contracts. This will help you check.
   5. *Consider notarization.* It's a good preventative; in fact, it's required for certain public filings. A notary attests to a signature's validity after witnessing the actual signing and reviewing proof that the signer is who he or she claims to be. The notary then affixes a notarial stamp or seal and signs and dates the document.
   6. *Don't forget your local document examiner.* Using high magnification and other techniques, they can analyze handwriting, paper, writing instruments, type, ink, language, grammar, and syntax to unmask a fake.

Now You See It, Now You Don't

Generally, the law will protect you from a paper swindler. A court won't hold you to a deal that you were tricked into signing. We attorneys call this *fraud in the execution*.

In addition, although you should avoid signing contracts with blank spaces, this doesn't give the other side the right to fill them in with terms to which you'd never agree. And if you ever worried about someone planting a time bomb in the fine print, consider Section 211 of the Restatement of Contracts: "Where the other party has reason to believe that the party manifesting such assent would not do so if he knew that the writing contained a particular term, the term is not a part of the agreement."

In a recent case, a company fired an employee but offered him $38,000 if he'd sign a general release they prepared. He took that release home and typed in, in a way that wasn't noticeable, this phrase regarding the claims he was giving up: "except as to claims of age discrimination and breach of contract." After the company countersigned, he sued them for (guess what) age discrimination and breach of contract. Imagine that! Ultimately, he lost. Would you be surprised if I told you that employee was an attorney? By the way, I bet the company won because it kept a copy of the unaltered release in its files.

The Offer You Can't Refuse

Remember the beginning of *The Godfather*, when Michael told Kay how Don Corleone closed a certain deal? "Luca Brasi held a gun to his head—and my father assured him that either his brains or his signature would be on the contract." This is a classic example of the legal doctrine of *duress*. A court won't hold you to a deal that you were forced into. Of course, there are compelling reasons not to litigate against the Godfather.

II

DEALS

WITHIN DEALS—

APPLYING THE

DEAL POWER

SYSTEM

7

PARTNERS:

WHO'S IN AND WHO'S OUT?

> If money talks, how come it's the "silent
> partners" in a business deal who do the
> financing?
>
> —Scott Thomson

Fred wanted to clear his conscience before he died. His longtime business partner, Jack, stood at his bedside. "Jack, I need to tell you that I stole $150,000 when you took that vacation in Italy a few years ago."

"Fred, let's not talk about this now," said Jack.

"And I was the one who mortgaged our office building to cover my gambling debts."

"Please, Fred, this is hardly the time . . ."

"And I," moaned Fred, "have been screwing your wife twice a week for the last twelve years!"

Jack looked at Fred gently. "Don't worry," he said, "I've known about all this for ages. Why do you think I poisoned you?"

∎ ∎ ∎

The relationship between partners, co-owners of an enterprise run for profit, is the most intimate one in the business world. Regardless of technical form, the duties of loyalty and good faith run very high. The sins of one are visited on the other, your partner's debts may become your own, and even the best contract can't completely protect you from a slothful or wayward co-venturer. Thus, it is with the greatest care that we invite others to join us as principals on our side of the negotiating table.

Figuring how to share a deal with others is a deal within a deal, a deal to structure a relationship that often arises when a business opportunity is first presented. So out comes our checklist, with some interesting variations and digressions.

STEP 1: STEP BACK (AND THINK)

Why a Partner? (Goals)

You've heard the saying "If something's worth doing, it's worth doing alone." So I ask again, "Why a partner?" Do you need money, credit, expertise, a property, contacts, or someone who can get to work right away? Maybe you need someone to complement you: They can schmooze, you like numbers; they're wildly creative, you're down-to-earth; they're disciplined and motivated, you're not.

Now, let's get personal. Do you love the camaraderie? Do you like bossing someone around? Are you scared to go it alone? As before, note all your needs, both the objective and the personal. This is the starting point for figuring who's in and who's out.

Will My Partner(s) Be Worth It? (Value)

Let's use the framework described in "Value: Will It Be Worth It?" on pages 9–14.

Dollar value. Weigh the dollar value of what they're bringing to the party. How much money will they help you make down the road?

Long-term potential. What do your partner(s) have that you haven't got? Assess their experience, skill, integrity, vision, motivation.

Subjective value. Do you like them? Do you respect them? Do you trust them? Is there special chemistry or troubling friction?

Risks. Is your partner-to-be a flake, a loose cannon, a cheat, or a fool?

Opportunity costs. Could you make more by yourself? Could you make more with other partners?

Transaction costs. How much time, energy, and money will it take to reach an understanding with your partner(s)?

What do your partner(s) want in exchange? And this leads right back to the bottom-line question: Will my partner(s) be worth it?

For additional insight, trade places with your prospective partner(s) and ask yourself these questions from their point of view. Also, use figure 1.5 on page 15 to create a mirror image of these inquiries: By *not* having a partner, what risks do I avoid, what other possibilities open up, what transaction costs do I save, what do I not have to give up, and how much money and other benefits will I lose?

What Else Can I Do?

Alternatives I: Hats

Don't assume that everyone wants to be a principal or co-owner. Partnership is just one way to structure the relationship among those on your side of the table. There are many others:

Lender. You may be far better off with a loan than with a partner. True, you may have to make periodic payments. However, interest may be tax-deductible, debt can leverage up your rate of return, and inflation means that loans are repaid in cheaper dollars. More importantly, once your creditors are repaid they will not share in the (presumably) unlimited growth of your endeavor.

Supplier. I use this term broadly. Just because someone has office space, a key piece of equipment, or a secret formula doesn't automatically mean they have to be your partner. You can still create a fair and profitable relationship as seller-buyer, lessor-lessee, or licensor-licensee.

Employee. Many prefer the comfort of a steady paycheck to the headaches of ownership. A potential employee's deal can be sweetened with life, disability, or health insurance; various pension plans; or other perks. A formal agreement stating they can only be fired *for cause* offers even more security. They can still share in the long-term success of an enterprise through some form of bonus plan, stock option, or performance-based compensation. On the other hand, if you want to keep it simple, hiring them as an independent contractor may be the way to go.

Target. If your potential partner is a company, maybe you should just buy that company outright?

Agent or broker. Someone who simply helps put your deal together might be happy with a (fat) commission and nothing more. Review the section on agents and brokers in Step 2 on pages 35–36.

Strategic ally. Companies and individuals often pursue mutually beneficial goals without hashing out a formal agreement. But here are two warnings: One, the law may still consider you partners for certain purposes. Two, certain arrangements between companies that control a large share of a given market may violate antitrust laws, so consider consulting an antitrust lawyer.

These common alternatives will help you: (1) better define everyone's roles; (2) avoid the entanglements and risks of taking on partners; and (3) keep more of the long-term upside for yourself. On the flip side, in certain deals you may prefer one of these roles for yourself. Work the creativity exercises on pages 15–24 to fine-tune them or come up with new ones.

Alternatives II: Legal Choice of Entity—Basic Menu

Until now I've used the term *partnership* as shorthand for working together as a team. This isn't technically accurate. Legally, there are many forms your business can take, a few of which I've already mentioned in the section on asset protection on pages 107–17. Lawyers usually think in terms of four basic ones:

A *sole proprietorship* is really just a fancy term for owning and running a business by yourself.

The *general partnership* is your garden-variety partnership, often defined as "an association of two or more to carry on, as co-owners, a business for profit."

The *limited partnership* consists of one or more general partners (which, for example, may be an individual, a corporation, or even a general partnership) who run the business and are liable for all of its debts, and one or more limited (silent) partners who are only on the hook for what they put in.

The *corporation* is a fictitious entity separate from its owners and managers. It can do business in its own name (like a "real" person), but its shareholders are only liable only for their investment.

Figure 7.1 contrasts many of the differences among these four. In practice, however, they're more alike than you might think. For instance, theoretically, corporations separate ownership (by shareholders) from management (by officers and directors); yet in closely held ones the shareholders often *are* the officers and directors. With a little planning a partnership can be structured to go on indefinitely and separate management from ownership just like a corporation. Although stock should be easier to sell than a partnership interest, a minority stake in a closely held corporation may be no more marketable. Also, in "Choosing the Right Entity: Part 1" on pages 114–17, we already saw how limited limited liability may actually be.

Anyway, regardless of form, you always have to address the big-picture issues listed in figure 7.2. And whether your partners are now called minority shareholders, limited partners, or something else (see below), the crisscrossing duties imposed by law demand a high degree of competence, good faith, and fair dealing from everyone.

Having said all this, there is one area in which your choice of entity is key: tax. For each entity, starting up, operating, and winding down will have different tax consequences, and often these are the real deciding factors. For one thing, corporations are subject to the infamous double tax, one on the corporation, another on the shareholders. Partnership income is taxed at the individual partner's rate, so to some extent, profits, losses, deductions, and credits may be shifted among the partners. The rules defy a neat summary. Even if they didn't, you'd still need expert help from an attorney or an accountant to plan intelligently.

Alternatives III: Legal Choice of Entity—Extended Menu
To round out our discussion of alternatives, here are a few other terms that you might hear:

A *joint venture* is merely a general partnership that's limited to a specific undertaking.

Joint tenancy and *tenancy in common* are really ways to take title to real property, not true forms of partnership, in and of themselves. The joint tenancy has a *right of survivorship*: When a joint tenant dies, all of his or her share goes to the remaining one(s); the dying joint tenant's heirs get nothing. Interests in a tenancy in common are inheritable. In both, each tenant shares nonexclusive possession of the entire property with the other(s).

Subchapter S corporations are popular because they are such a simple way to avoid the corporate double tax. As with a partnership, profits and losses pass through the S corporation directly to its shareholders. A special filing is required, and the number and types of shareholders and the classes of stock are restricted. Be careful: If the S corporation election is faulty, the individual returns of the shareholders may also be incorrect. By the way, regular corporations are sometimes called *C corporations*.

A hybrid between a corporation and a partnership, the *limited liability company* is all the rage today. Like a corporation, it's created by filing under state law, members are liable only for what they put in, and there may be more than one class of interests (stock). Like a

CHOOSING THE RIGHT LEGAL ENTITY

	Sole Proprietorship	General Partnership	Limited Partnership	Corporation
Who is personally liable?	The owner.	Each partner has unlimited liability for all partnership debts.	General partner has unlimited liability; limited partners only up to their investment.	Generally no one (but see page 114); each shareholder's liability is limited to their investment.
Who runs it?	The owner.	Majority rules, unless otherwise agreed. Generally, each partner can bind partnership with third parties.	General partners manage; limiteds may not participate.	Management is centralized in the board of directors.
What's it like raising money?	Simple. Owner provides it all; can seek loans.	Voluntary or mandatory contributions from partners. May trigger securities law. Also, loans.	Like general partnership, but issuing interests in a limited partnership triggers securities laws.	Complex. May have different classes of common or preferred stock, bonds, and other debt instruments. Subject to securities laws.

How expensive and complicated is it to set up?	Not very, but like any other business may need licenses, permits, name protection, etc.	Created by agreement; main expense is legal fees to prepare partnership agreement; can cost more than incorporating.	Like general partnership, also created by agreement. Must file certificate of limited partnership (at small cost). Securities law compliance may be expensive.	Complex: filing and legal fees to incorporate; must "qualify" to do business in other states; securities law compliance; hold and keep minutes of regular shareholders and director's meetings; pay annual franchise taxes.
How easy is it to transfer interests?	By definition, can't transfer ownership but can sell assets.	To admit a new partner and for one partner to transfer interest, all others must consent.	Unanimous consent required to add new partners. Also, in reality, limited partnership interests are not (for tax reasons) transferable.	Absent agreements to the contrary, shareholders can dispose of shares freely, if there's a market.
How long does it last?	Till owner dies or withdraws.	Technically, death or withdrawal of even one partner dissolves partnership.	Until withdrawal of a general partner or end of term stated in limited partnership agreement.	Perpetual.

Fig. 7.1

partnership, it usually terminates on the death or "withdrawal" (resignation, expulsion, bankruptcy, retirement, or the like) of a member, the transfer of a member's interest must be approved by everyone else, and for tax purposes profits and losses are allocable. It's managed either by its members or a third party, without the formality of officers and the board of directors, as in a corporation. Specific features may vary from state to state.

Finally, there are some esoteric choices: various forms of trusts (no longer fashionable), cooperatives, and unincorporated associations. See your business lawyer for details.

STEP 2: GET HELP

With a really easy partnership, such as a friendly 50-50 split between two on a simple project, you may get by on your own. However, once you start adding people, varying payouts, creating buyout provisions, defining roles, and fingering your menu of entities, plan for some detailed negotiations and paperwork and longer meetings with your professional business midwives: the lawyers and accountants. Among other things, you may need tax planning, state and federal securities filings, comprehensive partnership or shareholder agreements, as well as thorough due diligence. Review Step 2 to see if there are other kinds of experts or resources that may help.

Conflicts of Interest

When a small group of people all agree on exactly how they'll team up, they often hire one lawyer to draw up the papers. Although this can save time and money, it will deny each participant his or her own advocate and, consequently, his or her very best deal. Moreover, the attorney chosen will have a potential conflict of interest with each person in the room. With corporations, especially closely held ones, it's even trickier. Generally, once the corporation is born, it's the entity and not the individuals who conceived it that becomes the attorney's client. Yet it's those individuals, the directors, officers, and shareholders, who direct the lawyer. Thus, if you're involved in any of these situations and things get rocky, the original lawyer's conflict of interests may force him or her to withdraw completely, and each person will have to go out and hire his or her own new representative.

STEP 3: CHECK IT OUT

The only people you want to know better than those on the other side of the table are those on your own! Now is a good time to reread Step 3. Everything there applies here.

STEP 4: MINIMIZE RISK

In addition to the issues we already discussed in Step 4 (such as insurance and boilerplate), there are two areas that are especially important.

Control

Depending on your choice of entity, structuring your relationships so you can stay on top of or at least on an equal footing with your colleagues can be treacherous.

In Partnerships
For the most part, control in a general partnership is a question of agreement. Power and responsibilities might be shared or divided; approval on certain key issues, such as settling lawsuits, borrowing, or requiring additional capital contributions, might require a majority or supermajority vote, or even unanimous consent. It's up to those involved.

Limited partnerships are a different story. Basically, the general partners run the show. With certain exceptions for ailing businesses, limiteds ought not participate in management, lest they become liable as generals. Because the laws vary from state to state, if you are a limited, check carefully before stepping out of your role as a passive investor.

In Corporations
On the other hand, corporate control, which is governed by detailed state laws, is complex and intriguing. Although the directors and officers run the day-to-day business, it's the shareholders who approve major changes, such as mergers, dissolutions, amendments to the corporation's bylaws and articles of incorporation (which are essentially

the contract between the shareholders and the corporation), and many other matters prescribed by law, like the selection of attorneys and accountants to evaluate directors and officers, transactions in which management has an interest, and so on. To top it all off, shareholders have the right to elect or remove directors. Thus, shareholder voting rights are the ultimate units of power.

Against this Byzantine backdrop we find multifarious (and sometimes nefarious) stratagems, as participants jockey for corporate control. Here are some common ones:

A corporation can issue many *different classes of stock* with different payouts of higher or lower priority and/or greater, lesser, or even no voting rights.

Cumulative voting ensures that minority shareholders will have representation on a board of directors. It allows them to take votes they'd otherwise have to spread among a group of candidates and cumulate them on one director. Without it, they'd always be outvoted. Staggering the terms of directors, allowing the majority to boot one without cause, or simply reducing the size of the board are all ways to defeat cumulative voting.

Under *pooling agreements*, shareholders agree to vote their shares a certain way on certain issues. Generally, they're legal so long as they're not used to extend shareholder control beyond the limits generally imposed by corporate law.

Voting trusts and *irrevocable proxies* have similar effects. With the former, a trustee takes legal title to shares, which it votes on behalf of their beneficial (financial) owners. With the latter, shareholders simply grant someone else the authority to vote their shares.

The balance of power among corporate players can also be altered through increased quorum or voting requirements, arcane procedures for formal notice, cleverly chosen record dates for the closing of stock transfer books, informal or "inconvenient" director's and shareholder's meetings, stock recapitalizations, and all kinds of other subtle traps buried in the bylaws or articles of incorporation. Here's the bottom line: Failing to appreciate the practical effect of these little devices can lead to ugly surprises. If you're participating in a corporation, find a sharp corporate lawyer to look out for you.

Changing Members

In business, as in life, people come and go. Down the road, if you can't control who is on your team, then all your careful planning, investi-

gating, and risk management may be for naught. Here are three standard ways to handle the problem:

Preemptive rights protect corporate shareholders from the dilution of their financial and voting rights. Basically, these rights give them first dibs on newly issued shares. The same idea may also be applied to additional contributions to a partnership. Usually these rights are a question of agreement, though at times they're a matter of law. Be aware that preemptive rights can be a major inconvenience when you're trying to raise money quickly.

Transfer restrictions prevent the sale or transfer of interests in an enterprise to others. With corporations, such prohibitions must be printed right on the stock certificates. In partnership agreements, such restraints might be set out as nonassignment clauses or the requirement of unanimous consent to admit new or replacement partners.

Buyout agreements go hand in hand with transfer restrictions. They're triggered when a team member leaves either voluntarily, through resignation or retirement, or involuntarily, due to breach, physical or financial disability, or death. Common solutions include granting the corporation or certain partners or shareholders an option or a right of first refusal to buy the leaving member's interest, making such a purchase or sale an obligation of the remaining members or the entity, liquidation of the enterprise, or even a public offering. Valuing the leaving member's interest can be tricky. It may be decided in advance, for example, by formula, or by formal appraisal at the time. Reciprocal life insurance policies among key members, also known as partnership insurance, or policies held by the entity can provide the cash needed for unexpected buyouts.

Here are some other concerns: Will the leaving member sever all ties with the enterprise? Will they leave any intellectual property rights behind? Will they sign a noncompetition and/or confidentiality agreement? Settling these issues can get very sticky, especially if someone leaves on bad terms. From the venture's point of view, agreeing on all this up front would be better. On the other hand, if you're the one who wants to walk, the more hooks you have in your colleagues, the more concessions you'll be able to extract before you leave.

KEY ISSUES IN DOING BUSINESS AS A TEAM
(AN OVERVIEW)

OBLIGATIONS

What is each member contributing to the enterprise?

What are each member's continuing responsibilities?

SPLITS

How will each member participate in the profits?

How will the venture's assets (money, real property, equipment, intellectual property, goodwill) and liabilities be divided if it folds?

AUTHORITY

Which of the following decisions are to be made by one member, a majority, a supermajority, or unanimous consent?

- borrowing money
- signing checks
- declaring bankruptcy
- admitting new members
- settling lawsuits
- making members contribute more money
- selling or licensing assets
- hiring employees
- other key business decision

MEMBERSHIP CHANGES

When can a member be thrown out? What do they get to keep if that happens?

What happens if a member wants out on their own?

When can a new member be admitted? What must they do?

What happens when somebody dies or is disabled?

Fig. 7.2

STEP 5: NEGOTIATE

Negotiation is negotiation. So put the tips in Step 5 to good use. Take another look at figure 7.2, which flags the key questions to consider when organizing your team. For the moment, forget technicalities like tax, choice of entity, and other legal categories. Once you've agreed on the basics, the rest will fall into place, with a little help from your friendly neighborhood lawyer and accountant.

Also, think twice before you negotiate too aggressively with potential teammates. You don't want to start off a long-term relationship on the wrong foot.

STEP 6: WRITE IT DOWN

These arrangements require not only written agreements but often governmental filings like tax returns, incorporation papers, and securities compliance as well. So be prepared. You may be in for piles of paperwork. Review Step 6 for details.

8

MAKING DEALS WITH

PROFESSIONALS

In the multitude of counselors there is safety.
—Proverbs 11:14

Each time you hire one of the deal-making specialists, a banker, lawyer, accountant, detective, agent or broker, consultant, or appraiser to help you with a deal, you're cutting yet another deal within a deal. In Step 2 we inventoried their quirks and some of the special considerations in hiring them. Now we use the Deal Power System to bring them on board.

STEP 1: STEP BACK (AND THINK)

Why Hire a Professional? (Goals)

Admitting you need or can benefit from help is the single best thing any deal maker can do. That great battlefield of business is strewn with the corpses of buck privates and five-star generals alike who "should've asked."

Generally, you hire a professional because he or she can help you make a better deal, warn and protect you against potential problems, or perform a specific task you can't do yourself. In certain situations, a professional may even generate a deal. At other times, he or she might urge you to walk away.

But as always, there's a subjective dimension. Do you enjoy the camaraderie? Do you need an expert's reassurance? Do you feel stronger with powerful allies? Do you simply think you're supposed to? Go back to pages 7–8 in Step 1. As before, a little introspection can really sharpen your focus.

Is the Professional Worth It? (Value)

A professional should add value to your deal.

Dollar value. Will he or she negotiate a better price or terms for you? Will he or she give you the information you need to do the same? Will he or she alert you to pitfalls that could cost you money down the road?

Long-term potential. Is an ongoing relationship with the expert valuable in and of itself? Will he or she enhance the strategic value of your deal?

Subjective value. Can you learn from him or her? Is there special chemistry or troubling friction? Will he or she give you more credibility?

Risk. What if the professional is dishonest? What if he or she screws up? What if he or she is too slow or unavailable?

Opportunity costs. This all ties in to alternatives (see below). Is the effort and money spent on cutting a deal with one professional better spent on another, or not at all?

Transaction costs. How much time, energy, and money will it take to reach an understanding with your professional?

What does your professional want in exchange? Once again, this leads back to the bottom line: Is the professional worth it?

Evaluating a professional after the fact is also challenging. Many times you'll wonder if things wouldn't have gone just as well had you ignored advice, negotiated yourself, or hired someone else. When it comes to risk management, this is doubly true. You may have paid lots of money only to hear there's little to worry about. If you feel cheated, remember, you paid for peace of mind.

What Else Can I Do? (Alternatives)

Try some of the techniques we learned in Step 1 on pages 15–24. Here are four special things to think about as you consider potential candidates:

• *Know in which area you need help.* Today's shopping mall of expert support is noisy, crowded, and confusing. Bankers, attorneys, accountants, detectives, consultants, and others all vie for the deal maker's dollars. Functions overlap, expertise can be highly specialized, and certain professions play different roles, or none at all, depending on the industry. Take the time to learn what's out there. Like everyone else, professionals are hawking something. Before you buy, make sure you really need it.

• *Shop.* Some professionals are better than others. There's tremendous variation in ability, experience, and price, and just because your Aunt Minnie knows someone doesn't mean that someone's any good. Finding, meeting, and checking out help takes time, so start early, before there's a deal on the table and you're under the gun. Here are a couple of great questions to ask: "What distinguishes you from your competitors?" and "If I engage you, how will I evaluate your performance?"

• *Bigger doesn't mean better.* It may stroke your ego to hire the "big guns," but if your deal's too small to show up on their radar, you're begging for big bills and lousy service. Usually, large or prestigious firms work best with large or prestigious clients. And of course, the fancier the front, the fatter the fees. Leaner organizations may not have the technical support or menagerie of specialists but may offer greater personal attention, accountability, and economy. In fact, the true specialist is often not found at the large firm.

• *Don't forget self-help.* See pages 41–42.

STEP 2: GET HELP

• *Educate yourself.* Lots of great stuff has been written about how to hire and work with various professionals. Network with those who have experience hiring the same kind of expert you need.

• *Use one professional to find another.* Good professionals in one area often know good professionals in others. They like to refer because: (a) it makes them look good to their clients; (b) they'd rather work with another expert they respect; and (c) it generates cross-referrals. Nevertheless, check out the recommendation yourself. You never know when someone's trading favors or simply has poor judgment.

• *Is there a professional organization or an educational institution that can help?* This varies from specialty to specialty. They may help you find a candidate, evaluate performance, or pursue complaints.

STEP 3: CHECK THEM OUT

Give them the once-over. Unless you've got a real inside line (a well-connected friend in the same profession), it's tough to know how good any expert really is. Between the specialized jargon, polished facade, and professional ego, a layperson may be in for a serious snow job. Don't let yourself be intimidated. Remember, *you're* interviewing. Tell them what you need, pose the tough questions, and after you leave their office, ask yourself:

• *Did they treat you with respect?* Lousy people skills are never an asset, no matter how clever the expert. If they alienate you, they'll alienate others. Who you hire reflects on you.

• *Did they communicate well?* Do they or someone from their office return calls promptly? Do they *really* listen to you? Can they explain technicalities in plain English?

• *Do they really know your area?* This is the age of specialization. No professional does it all. Quiz them on your industry. Ask if they've worked with others like you. If the person is exceptionally bright, you may take a chance on a quick study with little or no experience in your area. But if you start feeling like a guinea pig, go elsewhere.

• *Can they see the big picture?* A good pro should not only see how they fit into the deal as a whole but how the deal fits into your life. Do they ask? They don't have to become your confidant, but they shouldn't miss the forest for the trees.

• *Were they candid about fees?* You're entitled to some straight talk about how much and how long, even if it's a gross guesstimate on the low end and the high end. More on this later.

• *Will they be available in an emergency?* How do they react when you ask for their home or car phone number?

• *Do they have an attitude about the other side?* Sometimes they do. Your deal shouldn't become a grudge match.

• *Do you have a good gut feeling about them?* How was their body language? Their tone of voice? Were they too glib? Too pushy? Too meek? What was the office like? How's the support staff? If something doesn't feel right, ask yourself why.

• *Did they promise you the moon?* This is a cheap ploy to get you in the door. Expect big bills and substandard service. Don't allow yourself to be taken . . . at least not *that* easily.

"Do" diligence. Consider more formal inquiry. It doesn't have to be a full background check, but at the very least . . .

• *Verify their credentials.* Where did they go to school? How long have they been at it? Where have they worked? You'd be shocked at how many phonies are out there. Contact licensing and other professional affiliations. See if they're current. Ask for more info on the professional's background, achievements, or failings. There's no excuse not to make a few quick calls. Be wary of hiring anyone working under another person's license. They might not be fully qualified, and the person they're working under may shirk responsibility.

• *Check references.* Of course they're biased, but see pages 53–54.

• *Ask around.* Can you find and talk to present clients? Better still, can you find and talk to *former* clients or employees? How do their colleagues rate your professional? What is your professional's reputation in their business community? Are they involved in charitable activities? Do they have financial or personal problems? Inquire discretely, but, as always, consider the source.

• *Find out who's really going to do the work.* This is especially important with large firms. You're schmoozed by the gray-haired eminence. You're serviced by the grunt associate. Having routine work done by less expensive personnel often makes sense. But if you expect someone special to handle your work, make that clear.

• *Have they published? Do they speak?* Then read, or go hear them.

• *Have they been written about?* If you're dealing with someone prominent, this may very well be the case. What can you learn at the library, on-line, or at the newsstand?

Watch for actual and potential conflicts of interest. Knowing your professional's true loyalties is easier said than done. No matter how shrewd your questions, sometimes you never get the whole story.

• *Obvious conflicts.* A real estate broker tries to represent both the buyer and the seller, a consultant gets a commission for the product he recommends, or an investment banker starts working with your competitor. Know that any trustworthy professional will disclose obvious conflicts right away.

• *Hidden conflicts.* The appraiser lowballs you because his brother-in-law wants to bid. An accountant betrays his professional standards to avoid losing a key client. Your lawyer winks at the other side because he's looking for business. There are as many ways to be taken by those on your side as there are deals to be made, and it takes an unusually penetrating mind to smoke these out. Hire carefully, be suspicious, consider second opinions, cultivate a network of business intelligence that will give you the inside dirt, investigate, and ask twice as many questions when your representative seems less than 100 percent committed to your agenda.

STEP 4: MINIMIZE RISK

Here is some of the best advice you can glean from Step 4:

• *If you can, try them out on something small first.* If you don't get along, better to find out on the first date than two years into the marriage.

• *Pay later, not sooner.* Don't be surprised if a retainer is required—it helps the professional check *you* out. Nevertheless, try to hold onto as much of your dough as possible until the services are complete. This will help eliminate the risk of being snookered and position you to negotiate a discount if the service was lousy.

• *Use conditions.* If your arrangement contemplates circumstances under which fees are reduced or not payable at all—for example, if your deal never closes—then spell out those conditions.

• *Assume they won't work out and plan for it.* Build in the right to cut them loose. Establish in advance what you'll owe. Have the phone number of an understudy in your Rolodex.

• *Stay in charge.* Keep your professionals on a short leash. Make it clear that they have no, or extremely limited, authority to bind you.

• *Find out if they're insured.* Most professionals have some kind of malpractice policy. Sometimes it's even required by law. Asking may be touchy, but if your professional drops the ball, you may need a deep pocket to recover.

See figure 8.1 for more tips.

15 WAYS TO GET THE MOST
FROM YOUR PROFESSIONALS

1. *Get them involved early.* A five-minute phone call may prevent five years of litigation. Get your professionals in the loop early, before you give away the store. If you can't, at least tell the other side that you'll need to run everything by your lawyer, banker, accountant, or other expert before you agree to anything.

2. *Don't waste their time.* Don't feel snubbed if they're abrupt. If they're any good, they're busy. Prepare for your phone calls and meetings. Keep your communication short and to the point. If you're an organization, designate a point person so the pro doesn't have to have the same conversation six times. Get them what they need, when they need it.

3. *If money is an issue, try to save them time.* Sometimes certain clerical or routine tasks can be performed just as efficiently by you as by your $250-an-hour expert. Many experts will be sensitive to your budget and will work with you on this.

4. *Question bills.* As Confederate statesman and lawyer Judah P. Benjamin used to say: "First I charge a retainer; then I charge a reminder; then I charge a refresher; and I charge a finisher." See pages 197–200. Find out what all those billing codes on your invoice really mean.

5. *Don't nickel-and-dime.* If the price is more or less fair, live with it.

6. *Pay your bills on time.* This is the best way to say "Thank you."

7. *If there's a problem, talk about it.* Expect your professional to be bright. Don't expect them to be psychic.

8. *Confront conflicts of interest.* If your professional had, has, will have, or may have any relationship with the other side, or an interest in the subject matter of your deal, or any other matter that may affect your transaction or your business, then have a frank discussion about whether he or she can represent you without bias as soon as you can. Honest professionals will be forthright and candid about their conflicts of interest.

9. *Communicate in writing.* Most professionals take written instructions far more seriously than spoken ones. They know your letters or memos may become key evidence in your malpractice suit

Fig. 8.1 *(continued on following page)*

Fig. 8.1 *(continued)*

against them. On the flip side, study every piece of correspondence you receive from them. Correct every inaccuracy in writing. Keep a record of your oral communications and confirm the important ones in writing.

10. *Keep good files.* Not only is this good evidence, but if you fire a professional in midstream, you can be up and running with a replacement *tout de suite.*

11. *Don't tell them how to do their job.* Don't withhold or distort information, compete, or play Mr. or Ms. Know-It-All. Let them do their thing. They may very well lay out much better options than you could ever dream up.

12. *Educate yourself.* The better you understand what the professional does, the more comfortable both of you will be. Read up.

13. *Ride herd.* Stay on top of your professionals by staying in touch. In large deals circulate a list with basic contact information and responsibilities. Don't let tasks fall between the cracks. Set a schedule in advance and keep everyone accountable.

14. *Don't undercut them.* Once you've hired someone to do your bidding, having backdoor conversations with the other side will weaken your professional's effectiveness.

15. *Remember who's boss.* They're working for you, not the other way around.

STEP 5: NEGOTIATE

Price is usually the one issue that everyone assumes is nonnegotiable. Not true. Many professionals will adjust their fees if you ask. This is especially true if you're throwing them lots of business. Here are the basic pricing structures you'll run into time and again.

• *Hourly or daily rates.* I believe there's an innate fairness to billing by time. The professional simply multiplies the time spent by their standard billing rate. An hour's pay for an hour's work, a day's pay for a day's work. But there is a built-in conflict: The longer it takes, the larger the fee. Prevent runaway bills by insisting that your professional get your express, prior, written approval before specific tasks are undertaken and check in with you or send you bills frequently enough so that you can control costs (or at least try to). Here are some other ways a pro can make two plus two equal five:

The minimum billing unit. I know of a lawyer whose minimum billing unit is the quarter hour. With a blizzard of two- or three-minute phone calls, he boasts that he can get in at 9:00 A.M. and bill eight hours by 10:15! Obviously, the smaller the minimum unit, the better. Routine tasks in common transactions may also be assigned a fixed amount, regardless of how quickly they're performed—for example, an attorney incorporating a company, or a private detective searching certain public records.

Double billing. When two or more hourly professionals start jaw-boning about your problem, it gets real expensive, real fast. Double billing may be legit when different specialists are needed. Other times, you're financing some rookie's education. Don't. Here's another boondoggle: The professional has down-time, such as travel or waiting time, for one client, during which they do work for another. If you're the client with the downtime, you may think this outrageous; on the other hand, you'll probably never find out.

Padded bills are common. After all, 8 3/4 hours could just as easily be nine, or even ten hours. It's a tough area to police. Know that in big firms there's lots of pressure on young members to bill hours. Watch for large round numbers. Question each entry. Keep track of time to the extent you can: phone calls, meetings you attend, and so on. Compare your numbers to the ones on your bill.

Bills that are too general. A two-line invoice for 226 hours begs for a detailed breakdown. It's every customer's right. And don't be surprised to find inaccuracies, double billing, padding, and the like. Many professionals present their initial invoice as a first offer. They'll cut fees, but only if their clients bust them on it.

• *The flat fee.* Certainty is the selling point here. You don't worry about runaway costs; the professional doesn't worry about billing questions. So far, so good. The problem, however, is in fixing the fee. Unless it's a standard service in a competitive market, the profession-als will protect themselves by quoting real high and excluding certain services. Otherwise, clients suck up too much time and treat them like the all-you-can-eat-salad-bar. So think twice before you agree to a flat fee. A well-controlled hourly may be better. And if you do opt for a flat, hold back enough cash to encourage your expert to finish the job. Here are some variations:

The retainer in its pure form is a set amount that assures some expert's availability for a certain period of time. Sometimes it's applied against hourly or other fees earned later. It may also refer to a returnable advance made for services to be rendered. It depends on the professional, so be clear.

Value billing is amorphous but now stylish, especially among lawyers. In essence, the fee is based on the value of the service to the client; sometimes it's negotiated in advance, other times after the fact. Obviously, it requires lots of good faith on both sides.

• *The percentage* is known by many names, including the commission, the contingency, and the cut. It's exactly what it sounds like: Your pro takes a piece of the action. It's how professionals make the big bucks.

When it's appropriate. Percentages work best when your representative is key to making the deal happen. If they help you sell, it makes them fight for top dollar. However, if they help you buy, there's a conflict of interest: The more you pay, the more they make. And if they do exactly the same thing they'd do if you'd hired them hourly, run the numbers to see which is better for you.

Whose deal is this anyway? Percentage deals can produce incredible windfalls, far, far in excess of any hourly fee . . . provided the deal closes. This can be a big problem. When the stakes get high, will your rep say no to a hefty commission just because the deal's mediocre for you? Also, will they finish what they've started once their check has cleared?

• *Bargaining tips.* Highly respected pros who work on percentage usually have the clout to withstand any attempt to cut their fees. But it never hurts to ask, especially when that pro is not the only game in town. Here are some other important considerations:

What's the percentage based on? Is it on everything you get or just a part, on gross or on net? If it's calculated on net, exactly which items are subtracted from gross to arrive at net? Also, if part of the percentage will be deferred or will not be in cash (for example, in stock), plan for this well in advance.

When is it payable? This will depend on the wording of your contract. Is it after the introduction has been made? After the deal has been negotiated? After the deal is signed? Be careful. You shouldn't have to pay a commission on a deal you reject.

How much is payable? Avoid paying a lump-sum commission up front. Let the middleman bear the same risk you do. Pay them over time in proportion to what you actually receive.

For how long is it payable? Certain deals go on for years. For example, a manager lands an actor a TV show that shoots for eight seasons, is syndicated, and even spins off into a new series with the actor as the star. Should the manager participate in all of it? Does your answer change if the actor boots the manager three months into the first season of the original show? Clauses that phase out commissions are sometimes called *sunset* provisions.

Is the contract written accurately? Make sure you or your lawyer pay scrupulous attention to the wording that describes commissions. The wrong choice of words could cost you big bucks.

• *The hybrid.* If none of these arrangements feel quite right, mix and match. Consider: an hourly rate against a percentage? A flat fee with an hourly if the job extends past a certain date? A percentage with a floor and a ceiling? A hybrid may take a little extra time to negotiate but may save you money.

• *Oh—by the way, that costs extra.* Of course you should know what is and is not included before your expert starts work.

Expenses. The list varies widely, from specifics like long-distance telephone calls to the engagement of expensive supporting professionals. These charges can really jack up your bill. As a rule of thumb, make items over a certain amount subject to your specific, prior, written approval and don't subsidize office overhead, such as inflated photocopy charges or separate charges for clerical work.

STEP 6: WRITE IT DOWN

Of course. But here, do it early, before the work starts, before you've paid a dime, and before time gets so tight you can't go elsewhere. Be especially clear about the professional's precise responsibilities.

9

WHEN BAD DEALS HAPPEN

TO GOOD PEOPLE

Better a bad agreement than a good lawyer.
—Italian proverb

Maybe you took a calculated risk and got tagged. Maybe you were lazy and skipped something. Maybe you did everything right and your deal went south anyway. "The best laid schemes o' mice and men / Gang aft a-gley," wrote Robert Burns. Now your challenge is to make the best of a bad situation. Let's examine the options.

RENEGOTIATION

The only permanent thing is change.

—Heraclitus

If your deal doesn't work anymore, see if the other side will let you change it. Use the Deal Power System to make a new deal. It should be much easier the second time around. After all, you already did most of the work (I hope) when you cut the deal in the first place.

• *Step back (and think).* Have your *goals* changed? What would bring more *value* to this deal? After you finish this chapter, consider the *alternatives* if you stay, as opposed to if you go.

• *Get help.* Do you need the same experts who helped you the first time? Is there a licensing, professional, or consumer group that can help you straighten things out? Have you talked the deal over with someone close to you?

- *Check it out.* What's really going on? Meet. Question. Inspect. Investigate. Audit.
- *Minimize risk.* Would restructuring or taking more control help? Can you get more security, collateral, or people on the hook? Would insurance make a difference?
- *(Re-)negotiate.* Set your bottom line. Assess your leverage. Work together on what's not working.
- *Write it down.* Get your amendments in writing, of course.

Thumb through the six steps for more ideas. Renegotiation is most likely to succeed when you have an ongoing relationship with the other side or are part of the same business community. In a true one-shot deal in which you're unlikely to deal with the other side again, it may be unrealistic. Your opponent has little incentive to accommodate you.

ALTERNATIVE DISPUTE RESOLUTION

> Discourage litigation. Persuade your neighbors to compromise whenever you can. Point out to them how the nominal winner is often a real loser—in fees, expenses, and waste of time. As a peacemaker, the lawyer has a superior opportunity of being a good man. There will be business enough. Never stir up litigation.
>
> —Abraham Lincoln

If renegotiation fails, most people assume that a lawsuit is their only option. However, ADR *(alternative dispute resolution)* is often the far more sensible first choice. It's usually cheaper, faster, more private, and better suited to creative problem solving than the courtroom. In fact, courts will sometimes insist that litigants try some form of ADR first. *Mediation* and *arbitration* are the best-known techniques, but there are others too.

Mediation

Think of mediation as negotiation with a moderator. The mediator is a neutral third party who listens, questions, clarifies, sets ground rules, and suggests alternatives, all to help the parties work out their own solution. A mediator has no authority to bind the parties, unlike an arbitrator, who does.

Because mediation is informal and nonadversarial and keeps disputants talking directly, it is surprisingly effective. Eastern cultures embrace it more readily. In China, for example, mediators settle thirty-five times as many disputes as the courts do. In the United States, studies show extremely high satisfaction rates on both sides and that mediated settlements are far more likely to be honored than litigated ones. In fact, experts say that mediation is successful 80 percent of the time. It's much cheaper and faster than litigation, and many disputes are settled in one sitting.

Mediation is a good choice when parties are cooperative, would like to preserve a relationship, just need to blow off steam, or want a creative solution that a court doesn't have the inclination or legal authority to grant (see page 213–14). Mediation probably won't work if one side is out for blood or too stubborn or far apart from the other.

Today there are hundreds of public mediation centers operating throughout the U.S., as well as numerous for-profit dispute-resolution services that offer mediation. Your mediator should be unbiased, experienced, and skilled. However, because there's currently no widely accepted certification or training for mediators, you may have to do a little extra shopping. Get recommendations from your lawyer or the local bar. Be wary of former judges: They're used to orchestrating or coercing settlements and may lack the diplomacy required of a good mediator. If your dispute involves technical knowledge, get a mediator with background in that field.

When one side wants to mediate and the other doesn't, an invitation directly from the mediator is more likely to bring the reluctant party to the table. For best results, each side should bring someone with the authority to settle, as well as an articulate and levelheaded spokesperson. Having people on your side with a calming influence, or that the other side really wants to talk to, is also good. If you're called on to make an opening statement, take it easy. Antagonizing the other side defeats the purpose of mediation.

Arbitration

Think of arbitration as "litigation lite" ($1/3$ the aggravation and $1/2$ the time). Essentially, the parties bring their quarrel to an impartial, private third party, who "makes an award" (renders a decision). Commercial arbitration goes way back to the Middle Ages. Unlike mediation, it involves a small informal trial.

At its best, arbitration combines the normal benefits of **ADR** (it is often cheaper, faster, less formal, and more private than litigation) with some additional advantages. Participants can argue their case forcefully, as they would in court, and since arbitration ordinarily is binding, they will have finality. You can choose arbitration at the time a dispute arises, or by writing it into your deal. Contract clauses requiring arbitration can list such specifics as the number of arbitrators, how they're chosen, the scope of the arbitration, the rules of evidence, and any limits on the arbitrator's power. The American Arbitration Association is the leader in the field, and contracts typically reference their rules as the ones that will apply.

To those on the brink of litigation, arbitration may sound awfully good, but there are plenty of horror stories. Arbitrators aren't bound by legal precedent and are rarely subject to judicial review. Their unfair or screwy decisions may be almost impossible to appeal. Arbitrators may be biased, they may overbill, or they may corruptly favor the party who sends them repeat business. Much due process and many of the procedural safeguards of litigation are omitted, sometimes resulting in the introduction of shoddy evidence and "trial by ambush." Often arbitration does not save either side time or money. It still involves expensive lawyers, with additional litigation costs if one party has to compel the arbitration, enforce an award, or appeal. So before you agree to arbitrate, think twice. You might be better off suing.

Variations

The mushrooming field of **ADR** offers other creative approaches that may be more appropriate to your circumstances:

• *Conciliation* is simply an informal meeting of the parties. A conciliator takes an even lighter touch than a mediator, often just bringing the parties together. The conciliator is not even supposed to make suggestions.

• *Early neutral evaluation* (ENE) is just what it sounds like. Each side presents their case to a neutral expert for an opinion on how well it would play in court. Predictably, settlement often follows.

• In *med-arb* (mediation-arbitration) you try to work things out by mediating but move to arbitration if you can't.

- The *rent-a-judge* approach is very popular in California. Parties pay a judge, who is granted customary authority but who uses a more flexible and expeditious version of normal courtroom procedure. You get the benefits of the system with a judge of your choice, who presumably has the time to attend to you.

- In a *minitrial* each party selects a principal, who hears a brief presentation of each side's case. A neutral moderator may preside. The disputants may be allowed to learn a little about each other's case in advance. Afterward, the principals meet and try to settle. Occasionally, the minitrial is spectacularly successful. For example, after three years of preparation and hundreds of thousands of dollars spent feuding over a complex patent infringement, TRW and Telecredit held a minitrial consisting of a six-week preparatory period and a two-day minitrial. The principals met and settled everything in thirty minutes!

An All-Purpose Warning

Often, there's little to lose by trying some form of ADR first. After all, you can always sue later. But here's one warning that applies not only to ADR but to any kind of settlement negotiation: In the hope of burying the hatchet, you may reveal much about your case that could damage you if you later end up litigating against the other side. If that risk is too great, reconsider ADR. Alternatively, if you're the one who has more to lose in this regard, get the other side to agree from the start that all statements will be considered *settlement negotiations*, which are inadmissible as evidence at trial, and that neither side will call the mediator, conciliator, early neutral evaluator, or similar functionary as a witness. This won't eliminate the problem, but it'll help.

Finally, know that many lawyers don't like ADR in whatever form. Sometimes it's unfamiliarity. Sometimes it's greed; it's bad for business. Sometimes it's strategic; some trial lawyers think even suggesting ADR is a sign of weakness (though it doesn't have to be). And of course, there are those personality types that live and love to litigate. In any event, you won't get pumped up about going to court after you read the next section.

LITIGATION

As a litigant, I should dread a lawsuit beyond almost anything short of sickness and death.

—Judge Learned Hand

"A piece of paper blown by the wind into a law court may in the end only be drawn out again by two oxen," say the Chinese. A Spanish Gypsy curse: "May you have a lawsuit in which you know you are right." Voltaire wrote, "I was never ruined but twice—once when I lost a lawsuit and once when I gained one." I could fill a whole chapter with quotes like these. There's little in business life more exasperating, infuriating, and aggravating than a lawsuit.

Why Litigation Should Be a Last Resort

Getting to Trial Takes Forever
Courtroom congestion is awful and getting worse all the time. Studies tell us that about 20 million civil cases are filed in the United States each year, with four times that many predicted by the year 2020. Notwithstanding the tort reformers (those who wish to establish caps on fees and awards in tort cases), business lawsuits make up the largest number of cases and the greatest portion of the backlog in the federal courts. Overbooked courtrooms and last-minute rescheduling are common. You may wait years just to get to trial.

Litigation Drags On and On and On
It isn't just sheer volume that chokes our courtrooms. Legal procedure is unimaginably technical and cumbersome. On the one hand, the rules level the field; on the other, they subject every move to intense and time-consuming scrutiny, argument, and documentation. According to former California attorney general Evelle J. Younger, "An incompetent attorney can delay a trial for months or years. A competent attorney can delay one even longer." See figure 9.1.

Litigation Costs Big Bucks
Business lawsuits tend to be hourly affairs; your high-powered legal tools are on the meter. Even a baby lawsuit will cost a few grand. If the litigation is complex, you'll need a team of lawyers. At $100, $200,

$300, $400, $500, or even more per hour *per attorney*, plus costs for paraprofessionals, expert witnesses, court reporters, travel, etc., you won't enjoy picking up the check.

Litigation Is Nasty

You're not making deals anymore. You're at war. Each side takes its most obnoxious stance, puffing up claims, distorting the truth, and vilifying the other. Day after day, you drag yourself to the battle-field, a forbidding courthouse filled with long lines, hostile clerks, and stony judges. Arbitrary deadlines interrupt your schedule. Spite-ful exchanges work your last nerve. Worry ruins your sleep. Your privacy is violated with impunity. Your time, your very life, is no longer your own.

You Could Lose

Imagine that! As in war, the outcome is never certain. Every day juries return ever loonier verdicts. So, depending on which side you're on, add to all of the above aggravations the potentially gratuitous indignity of having to fork over big bucks to your archrival. Your opponent may "recover," but will you?

To Sue or Not to Sue

Still there are times when your only choice is to sue. But before you pull the trigger, calm down and ask yourself the following:

Have You Missed the Legal Deadline?

Statutes of limitations set time limits on how long you can wait until you sue. For example, in California you have two years from the day an oral agreement is breached, four years for a written one, and three years from the date you discover fraud. If there's no statute of limitations on point, the doctrine of *laches* may do the same thing. If you've been napping on your rights to the point that your defendant no longer has a fair chance of defending, perhaps because evidence is unavailable or witnesses have died, the court may throw out your case. Sometimes a sharp lawyer can get around these roadblocks. More often, if you wait too long, you'll give up your day in court. End of discussion.

Can You Get Blood from a Stone?

Do a background check on your target's finances. Your defendant may be judgment-proof simply because they're broke or uninsured. Or they may have shielded their assets from a lawsuit so effectively that you'll never see a dime. Review the section on asset protection on pages 107–17. Either way (and as much as it pains you), you may want to let the whole thing go, unless, of course, you're looking for relief other than money (see page 214).

What Are Your Chances of Winning?

For this, you need some heavy-duty legal analysis, including a frank assessment of your case's strengths and weaknesses. Your attorney should factor in everything from procedural problems like finding and serving all the parties you need, to substantive issues such as whether the law is for or against you, to strategic concerns, including whether you're inviting a counterlawsuit. Remember that you must prove not only liability but damages (how much money you lost) as well.

Pray for sound, honest advice, because unless you're a lawyer, or exceptionally well informed, it's hard to know whether your litigator is telling the truth or throwing you a sales pitch. Consider a second or third opinion. Once you file, it's expensive, inconvenient, and damaging to switch lawyers midstream.

How Much Will It Cost?

Sometimes business litigation is about principles, but mostly it's about money. You want to win, but at an acceptable cost. Thus, on one side of the equation goes your guesstimate of what it'll cost (always more than you think). On the other goes your likely recovery, multiplied by the odds of your winning, and discounted by two other factors: inflation and the time value of money. In other words, $100 three or four years from now is worth far less than $100 today.

Even when the numbers don't justify it, sometimes you can't afford *not* to sue. For example, those who don't vigilantly defend their trademark rights may lose them. There's also your general reputation. Act like a wimp and the bullies will line up to get you.

How Committed Are You?

Don't underestimate psychic and opportunity costs. We discussed the former when we introduced the topic of litigation just a few pages back. You'll feel the latter every time you or someone in your company picks up the phone, takes a meeting, is deposed, or spends valuable time poring over court papers. After all, you could all be out making other deals. Be honest with yourself: Do you have the resolve, the nerve, and the patience to see it through?

Offense or Defense

Reverse the above five questions when you're the target of a lawsuit. Consider the statute of limitations, laches, and every other plausible defense. Evaluate the strength of your case and the cost of defense. But don't wait till a lawsuit has been filed to start your asset-protection program. Read the section on fraudulent conveyance on pages 108–109 and you'll see why.

Know that in real-life business disputes both parties often have legitimate claims against each other. So, if you're going to fight, you might as well throw the first punch. You'll seize certain tactical advantages, usually the first and last word at trial, and make the other side look petty and vindictive when they sue you back.

What to Do Before the Litigator Arrives

Many problems deal makers face in litigation originate with the way the wording of the formal contract was or was not negotiated. Ideally, that's where litigation planning starts. Your litigator will love you forever if your contract has boilerplate that gives you a leg up, such as your opponent having waived important rights, or your having the best choice of forum and state law. Review "The Airtight Contract" on pages 100–107. In the real world, however, too much attention to these issues can queer a deal. Try to get early tactical advantages through the formal contract, but don't beat yourself up with 20/20 hindsight if you didn't. The deal was your first priority; potential legal warfare, your second.

Once a deal starts getting rocky, you can usually see a lawsuit coming. Consider renegotiation and ADR. But since you may end up in court anyway, don't forget to stack the deck in your favor with these strategies:

Protest

Put your complaints in writing. Send notices via Federal Express or certified mail or in a similar way that generates receipts. Now that you're really going on the record, watch it. Anything you say, or don't deny, may be used against you. Add the following legal mantra to any exchanges with the other side: "This letter is not a complete statement of my rights and remedies, all of which I hereby expressly reserve." As you may gather, it'll let your attorney correctly restate your position later for maximum effect.

Preserve Evidence

Being right is one thing, proving it quite another. Prepare your case ahead of time:

- Accumulate a big fat file of receipts, letters, bills, and other documents; wherever possible, keep originals.
- If you can, get copies of what the other side's got in its files.
- Pay by check; it's good for your records and may lead you to the other side's bank accounts. You can even note disagreements or conditions on the checks. See also page 168.
- Take careful notes of all events and conversations; keep a diary or write memos to your file.
- Take pictures or videotape of any physical items or locations that may be under dispute.
- After the fact, locate key witnesses. Before the fact, bring along your own.
- Consider getting damage appraisals.
- Store anything you might use as physical evidence.

Before you visit your attorney, put everything together in a detailed blow-by-blow chronology. Give your lawyer a copy; it'll make him or her so happy and save you time and money. Be completely candid with your lawyers. If you withhold information, you're setting them up to be blindsided.

Call Your Litigator ASAP

Once you're in a dispute, actions that seem harmless—for example, your cashing the other side's check or ignoring a nasty letter—can really hamstring you later. An experienced litigator will tell you early on what you should and shouldn't do for maximum legal strategic advantage. This is especially true for large companies. Among other things, a good trial lawyer can help prevent the circulation of damaging internal correspondence which might later be used against the company in court.

Hiring an Attack Dog

Once again, you're making a deal, so use the Deal Power System. Review Chapter 8 and pages 25–28 in Chapter 2. With trial attorneys, there are a few special wrinkles:

For starters, beware of the Rambo litigator. Your advocate should be sharp, articulate, and assertive, have a thick skin, and know how to be obnoxious, if required. But a trial lawyer who's blatantly hostile, insanely competitive, and morally tone-deaf and otherwise exhibits all the harmful side effects of a testosterone overdose is a menace. That they lose the respect of their colleagues may not trouble you, but once they start alienating judge and jury, you've got a problem.

A number-one complaint against attorneys is that they don't return phone calls. When you're closing a deal this can kill you, but once you're in the middle of a suit, it's usually more annoying than damaging. Litigation marches to its own drummer. You may want a full-court press or a simple update, but the busy litigator knows that the important stuff happens on the court's schedule, not the client's. So don't fret if your lawyer doesn't call you back right away. In any event, it's your lawsuit, and the attorney who ignores a client's instructions is asking for a malpractice claim.

As we've seen, bias is built into every fee arrangement you make. Trial attorneys' fees are no different. If the lawyer is hourly, the longer things drag out, the more they make. If they're on a contingency, they'll balance maximum recovery against minimum effort. If they've run through their cap, they'll want to give you and your case the bum's rush. Even though filthy lucre should not influence your litigator's judgment, it probably will. So, factor this in when you evaluate their advice, especially when it comes to settling.

Settlement: "Liti-gotiation"

Ironically, despite all the time, money, and aggravation involved in bringing a lawsuit, the vast majority of cases settle. Usually, litigation is just a highly ritualized, aggressive, and expensive form of negotiation focused on a simple gamble: Who's going to win in court?

You'll be able to apply most of what you learned in Step 5 here. However, the mollifying prospect of some ongoing relationship is gone. Take another look at figure 5.1 on page 120: "Figure It Out: Who's Got the Clout?" Above all, litigation is a test of wills; to paraphrase the celebrated negotiator Herb Cohen, victory lies in the projection (or illusion) of "awesome power and the will to use it." As key moments arrive, such as the denial of a motion to throw out the case, the discovery of critical evidence, or the day before trial, posturing gives way to a cost-benefit analysis of war vs. peace, and bottom lines shift. The warriors tire. Neither side wants to be the first to utter the "S-word": settle. Yet nine times out of ten, that's exactly what someone does.

The Peace Treaty: Your Settlement Agreement

When you settle you cut yet another deal. Each side agrees to release its legal claims against the other pursuant to a nonaggression pact of their design. Because settlements are born of strife, suspicion, and depleted nerves, there are some special things for you and your lawyer to remember:

• Get your settlement agreement in writing. In many cases oral settlement agreements are not legally enforceable.

• Get it before you dismiss your suit.

• Get it fast, before someone changes their mind.

• Check with other legal specialists. A bankruptcy or tax lawyer, for example, may know things your litigator doesn't.

• Be scrupulously accurate about who's releasing who from which claims. Otherwise, you could give up important rights, or leave out parties who'll come after you later. Consider whether the release should be limited to the claims each side knows about at the time, or whether it will extend to claims that may later be discovered.

• Make sure the other side is represented by a lawyer or waives that right in writing. Courts will consider this if your opponent tries to reject the settlement by claiming they didn't realize what they were doing.

• Include language that makes it clear that you're not admitting any liability just because you're settling.

• Consider a confidentiality clause. You may not want the world to know the terms of your settlement agreement.

• Put as much muscle in your release as you can. Review Step 4. Look for guaranties, collateral, and airtight boilerplate. Tough lawyers may even have the other side *stipulate* to a judgment. If the other side reneges on the settlement, the lawyer can skip the trial and start seizing (or selling) their assets right away.

• Make sure the settlement is signed by someone with authority. Otherwise your opponent has an easy way to set it aside.

Winning?

To the lucky litigant who refuses to settle and toughs it out goes a *judgment*—a piece of paper memorializing the court's final decision. Usually, that means the loser pays the victor money *damages,* which may include interest, court costs, attorneys' fees, and even punitive amounts. Other times, the court may order the *restitution* of money or property; *specific performance,* which forces one or more parties to honor a deal; *rescission,* which cancels a deal; *reformation,* which is a rewriting of the contract to reflect what the court thinks the parties really meant; and/or an *injunction,* which stops a party from doing something. A judgment may even award some combination of the above or some other remedy closely related to the above.

All this may sound great in theory. In practice, when it comes to finding and seizing your defendant's money, the court is of limited help. Basically, you're on your own. And if you want to remind yourself of how maddening this can be, reread the section on asset protection on pages 107–117.

Sometimes there are happy winners in litigation. But I'd be surprised to find many who still wouldn't grumble about the time, money, and hassle of getting what they deserved all along. Even though judgments may be valid for decades, most trial attorneys have at least one drawer filled with ones they'll never be able to execute. Maybe that's why Ambrose Bierce defined litigation as "a machine which you go into as a pig and come out of as a sausage."

THE LIFE CYCLE OF A LAWSUIT

"In the beginning . . ." the litigants spend months filing *complaints, answers, amendments, counterclaims, cross-claims, demurrers, motions to quash, motions to transfer, motions to strike,* and so on, in order to define the basic who, what, where, and when of the case.

Then comes *discovery*, during which each side is given broad license to explore and test the other's case. Discovery was supposed to expedite settlement and avoid unfair surprises at trial. Instead, according to Walter K. Olson, author of *The Litigation Explosion*, it "provide[s] a near-inexhaustible repertoire of ways for litigants to tease, worry, irk, goad, pester, trouble, rag, torment, pique, molest, bother, vex, nettle and annoy each other." In minutes, paralegals punch out form *interrogatories* and *requests for admission*, written questions that take weeks to answer. Each side makes a point of taking the *deposition* of witnesses the other side doesn't want to involve. There may be irritating *inspections*. Lawyers harass each other with *notices to produce documents* (always at the most inconvenient times), literally burying each other in paper. It's siege warfare with office supplies.

Finally we get to trial. Whole weeks are lost just to jury selection. Innumerable witnesses drone on and on and on as lawyers examine, cross-examine, direct, redirect. More motions. More paper. Objection! Objection! Objection! At last, a decision comes back. Are we done yet? Of course not; there are the appeals! Round and round we go. When does it end?!

And these are just the routine *procedural* problems! Add to all this the challenge of actually applying the *substantive* law, those centuries of dusty statutes and cases that are often poorly worded and even more poorly decided, to the facts of your case. As your business problem festers, legal minds will split hairs trying to reconcile your problem with that entire enormous and riotous mosaic of Western jurisprudence. I hope you enjoy theoretical discussions. You'll be hearing a lot of them.

Fig. 9.1

BIBLIOGRAPHY

Argenti, Paul A., editorial director. *The Portable MBA Desk Reference: An Essential Business Companion.* New York: John Wiley & Sons, 1994.

Bloch, Ernest. *Inside Investment Banking.* Homewood, IL: Dow Jones–Irwin, 1986.

Bryant, Keith L., Jr., and Henry C. Dethloff. *A History of American Business.* Englewood Cliffs, NJ: Prentice Hall, 1983.

Clifford, Denis, and Ralph Warner. *The Partnership Book: How to Write Your Own Small Business Partnership Agreement.* Berkeley: Nolo Press, 1991.

Cohen, Herb. *You Can Negotiate Anything.* Secaucus, NJ: L. Stuart, 1980.

The Complete Book of Money Secrets. New York: Boardroom Classics, 1991.

Dary, David. *Entrepreneurs of the Old West.* New York: Alfred A. Knopf, 1986.

Dawson, Roger. *You Can Get Anything You Want (But You Have to Do More Than Ask).* New York: Simon & Schuster, 1985.

Delaney, Kevin J. *Strategic Bankruptcy: How Corporations and Creditors Use Chapter 11 to Their Advantage.* Berkeley: University of California Press, 1992.

Desmond, Glenn M., and Richard E. Kelley. *Business Valuation Handbook.* Los Angeles: Valuation Press, Inc., 1989.

Dychtwald, Ken. *Bodymind.* New York: Pantheon Books, 1977.

Eberle, Robert F. *Scamper: Games for Imagination Development.* East Aurora, NY: D.O.K. Publishers, 1987.

Eccles, Robert G., and Dwight B. Crane. *Doing Deals: Investment Banks at Work.* Boston: Harvard Business School Press, 1988.

Elgin, Suzette Haden. *Success with the Gentle Art of Verbal Self-Defense.* Englewood Cliffs, NJ: Prentice Hall, 1989.

Fisher, Roger, William Ury, and Bruce Patton. *Getting to Yes.* New York: Penguin, 1991.

Givens, Charles J. *Financial Self-Defense*. New York: Simon & Schuster, 1990.

Goldstein, Arnold S. *Asset Protection Secrets*. Deerfield Beach, FL: Garrett Publishing, Inc., 1993.

Henderson, M. Allen. *How Con Games Work*. Secaucus, NJ: Citadel Press, 1985.

Hoffman, Paul. *The Deal Makers: Inside the World of Investment Banking*. Garden City: Doubleday & Company, Inc., 1984.

Kellogg, Irving, and Loren B. Kellogg. *Fraud, Window Dressing and Negligence in Financial Statements*. Colorado Springs: Shepard's/McGraw-Hill, Inc., 1991.

King, Dennis. *Get the Facts on Anyone*. New York: Macmillan, 1995.

Lovenheim, Peter. *Mediate, Don't Litigate: How to Resolve Disputes Quickly, Privately, and Inexpensively Without Going to Court*. New York: McGraw-Hill, 1989.

MacCrimmon, Kenneth R., and Donald A. Wehrung. *Taking Risks*. New York: The Free Press, 1986.

Marshall, John F., and M. E. Ellis. *Investment Banking and Brokerage: The New Rules of the Game*. Chicago, IL: Probus Publishing, 1994.

McCarthy, Michael J. *Mastering the Information Age*. Los Angeles: Jeremy Tarcher, Inc., 1991.

McCormack, Mark H. *What I Should Have Learned at Yale Law School: The Terrible Truth About Lawyers*. New York: Avon Books, 1988.

———. *What They Don't Teach You at Harvard Business School: Notes from a Street-Smart Executive*. New York: Bantam Books, 1984.

McIntyre, William S. IV, and Jack P. Gibson. *101 Ways to Cut Your Business Insurance Costs Without Sacrificing Protection*. New York: McGraw-Hill, 1981.

Michalko, Michael. *Thinkertoys: A Handbook of Business Creativity for the 90s*. Berkeley: Ten Speed Press, 1991.

Moran, Robert T., and William G. Stripp. *Dynamics of Successful International Business Negotiations*. Houston: Gulf Publishing Company, 1991.

Nierenberg, Gerard. *Fundamentals of Negotiating*. New York: Hawthorn/Dutton, 1973.

Nierenberg, Gerard, and Henry H. Calero. *How to Read a Person like a Book*. New York: Pocket Books, 1973.

Ostberg, Kay. *Using a Lawyer . . . and What to Do If Things Go Wrong: A Step-by-Step Guide*. New York: Random House, 1990.

Passman, Don. *All You Need to Know About the Music Business*. New York: Prentice Hall Press, 1991.

Phillips, Michael, and Salli Rasberry. *Honest Business*. New York: Random House, 1981.

Ray, Don. *A Public Records Primer and Investigator's Handbook*. Burbank: ENG Press, 1991.

Rothfeder, Jeffrey. *Privacy for Sale: How Computerization Has Made Everyone's Private Life an Open Secret*. New York: Simon & Schuster, 1992.

Santoro, Victor. *The Rip-off Book*. Port Townsend, WA: Loompanics Unlimited, 1984.

Schachner, Robert W., with Marvin Quittner, Esq. *How and When to Be Your Own Lawyer: A Step-by-Step Guide to Effectively Using Our Legal System*. Garden City Park: Avery Publishing Group, 1993.

Schilit, Howard M. *Financial Shenanigans: How to Detect Accounting Gimmicks and Fraud in Financial Reports*. New York: McGraw-Hill, 1993.

Shenson, Howard L. *How to Select and Manage Consultants: A Guide to Getting What You Pay For*. Lexington, MA: Lexington Books, 1990.

Siver, Edward W. *The Executive Guide to Commercial Property and Casualty Insurance*. Chicago: Crain Books, 1981.

Tannen, Deborah. *Talking from 9 to 5: How Women's and Men's Conversational Styles Affect Who Gets Heard, Who Gets Credit, and What Gets Done at Work*. New York: William Morrow, 1994.

Thompson, Robert B. "Piercing the Corporate Veil: An Empirical Study." *Cornell Law Review* vol. 76 (1991): 1036.

Tobias, Andrew. *The Invisible Bankers: Everything the Insurance Industry Never Wanted You to Know*. New York: Simon & Schuster, 1982.

Train, John. *Famous Financial Fiascos*. Narration by Nelson Runger. New York: Bedford Research, Inc., by arrangement with Clarkson N. Potter, 1985. Audiocassette.

Tufts, Robert R., consulting ed. *Drafting Agreements for the Sale of Businesses*. 2nd ed. Berkeley: California Continuing Education of the Bar, 1988.

Tufts, Robert R., and Twila L. Foster, eds. *Drafting Agreements for the Sale of Businesses*. 2nd ed., updated June 1994. Berkeley: California Continuing Education of the Bar, 1994.

Ury, William. *Getting Past No*. New York: Bantam Books, 1993.

Vlahos, Olivia. *Doing Business: The Anthropology of Striving, Thriving and Beating Out the Competition*. New York: Franklin Watts, 1985.

Yeager, Wayne. *Status for Sale*. Los Angeles: Charter Publications, 1992.

Index

Entries in *italics* refer to figures.